HONESTY: THE FINAL FRONTIER
(Examining the Disharmony between Religion and Reality)

KEN DAHL

Copyright © 2016 Ken Dahl
All rights reserved.

ISBN: 1532758235
ISBN 13: 9781532758232

Foreword by Jim High

We live in an exciting time, a time of extreme change brought on by our ever increasing knowledge of Life, our Earth and the Universe. Ken Dahl's latest book addresses this change in the most appropriate way possible, with honesty.

In the ancient past humans understood almost nothing about the world they lived in, and they had almost no contact with humans outside their own culture or in faraway places. So they invented Gods who made sense to them about how the world works. That is why there are so many different ideas about all the Gods men have created around the world. Many thousands of years later these invented religions with their many Gods, or the single God of Judaism, Christianity and Islam, still rule the thoughts of the vast majority of people because the religions that grew in those ancient times became institutions that continually need to be fed (supported) by their members.

But two things have now greatly changed. Science and knowledge are answering all the questions, one by one, and the world is getting so much smaller that the various religions are bumping into one another with disastrous results. Isn't it time that we humans RE-THINK all these many God concepts? If those ancient people invented religious narratives that served them well, why can't we do the same today? Ken Dahl believes we can and that we should.

In this very generation a new definition of 'God' is being determined by millions of rational-thinking people. But that is the one thing most religions can't seem to even think about. Of course it is the one thing they absolutely must do if they are to survive. If you say you believe in God, then you must define what your God is. Personally, I did that long ago and define what others call God as the Life Force Energy of the Universe, or the Process of Life, or just Nature, or opening your eyes to the observable reality all around us as Ken Dahl talks about in this insightful book.

The world will come around to understanding this new situation, but only when religious institutions realize that their mission is not to prepare people for an eternity in some heaven with a God, but for one's own eventual death, and the optimistic, meaningful possibility of making this world a better place for their descendants.

What we need is an entirely new way of understanding what that thing we call God actually is. God is no longer that character described, worshiped, and feared in the Bible, but is the very Life Force Energy of the Universe itself. The old, ancient God concepts are holding us back from the truth of the reality in which we actually find ourselves.

The religions of this world seem to be stuck and afraid to let their beliefs evolve into something new and more in line with reality. But that is what mankind has always done throughout the entire history of the world. So our job is to break the log jam in our present thoughts about religion, God, and life itself, and let the new ideas and concepts about these things emerge as they will.

Ken Dahl's newest book, *Honesty: The Final Frontier / Examining the Disharmony between Religion and Reality* sets out to break this logjam and I highly recommend it to you. And based on this quote from Albert Einstein I am betting that if he were alive today he would too. "True religion is real living; living with all ones soul, with all ones goodness, all ones honesty."

- Jim High: President of SPAFER (Southern Progressive Alliance for Exploring Religion - www.spafer.org)

*This book is dedicated to my
soul synergist friend and mentor,
Lori Tolson,
whose words & wise counsel
have made such a
significant impact in my life.*

Prelude

Wow. I am so ... relaxed now. Yes, that's the word. Relaxed. And now that I am thinking and talking about it, that's really what I've always longed for my entire life. To just lean back and genuinely allow life to be what it is. It actually feels funny to me now that we should even have to have such a conversation. But we do…

I am not a shock jock, and have no need to evoke any sort of undue attention simply for the sake of writing something shockingly-entertaining. All I ask of my readers is this – if you read something here that comes across as unsettling or even disturbing, please take some personal time and brutal inner honesty to ask yourself WHY? Likewise, do the same with the subjects that resonate positive with you and your personal experiences.

That's all I ask.

One

THE FOREST THROUGH THE TREES

Albert was an older version of a 55-year-old man. At least that's what I thought at age 15. He worked in the iron mines and attended Our Savior's Lutheran Church at least twice a year, on Christmas and Easter. But more importantly, an envelope arrived on the first of each month "from the pastor's desk," with self-addressed envelope enclosed. A set amount that this "elderly couple" had decided on was promptly written out in the form of a check, and the flag on the mailbox went up at the end of their well-kept gravel driveway. This made God happy, and it seemed to feel right to Albert and his wife. He was a welder by trade, and a good one. And like any welder in those days he had all the equipment in his garage to weld pretty much anything that needed fixing around the farm. But what stood out the most about this neighbor was his pipe smoking in the winter time. I can still smell that sweet aroma of Carter Hall tobacco merging gently into the molecules of northern Minnesota's crisp, December air.

A vintage art print of a father and his son fishing among the lily pads hung on the wall in their porch. In the foreground a large bass had catapulted itself up out of the water with one of those traditional red and white wooden lures hanging off his lower lip. A plastic countertop radio played country music in the kitchen, but no one ever really sang along. It was just, well, the way things were in this rural community. I first heard the Beatle's *White Album* in their living room with my friend David as it played on their 200-pound solid oak high-fidelity stereophonic record player. I can still recall the dust particles floating in the beams of morning light as the song *Rocky Raccoon* was forever carved into the hard drive that is my brain. Why do I remember such events so vividly? And why do they seem so significant?

My adolescent years were "filmed" with a backdrop of neighborhood hockey rinks, Wolf Man Jack on the radio, snowmobiles, banana seat bicycles, first kisses at the drive-in theater, spearing fish with my buddies in the spring, and stealing alcohol from my friend's dad. My heart always sensed so many of these seemingly-meaningless stories as being important events that I was supposed to be paying attention to, but didn't. There was an undefinable simplicity to the world I was growing up in. It was all so loud, so colorful, so powerful, indeed mystical, but because of other voices it was all mentally rendered as nothing more than background scenery, or better put, the stage props for "the real play" that was taking place. And for me that so-called real play was a perpetual study of "life" according to a Holy book called "The Bible," and the many unquestionable doctrines of the church.

However, when I reminisce of younger days my fond memories are not of church meetings or doctrine-based explanations for every natural aspect of life, but things like going fishing with my dad, skipping school to visit the Sunrise Bakery, Mom's barley soup, and the amazing tree fort I made with my grade school friends. In my early twenties, one of my stoner pals named Gary had an old Oldsmobile 98, a beater of a car with holes that had been cut out in the floorboard for ice fishing purposes. The first time I watched him measure where to auger two holes in the ice at precisely 2 feet and 11 inches apart I was puzzled… until he removed the floor mats and drove his whale of a vehicle over them, perfectly aligning the holes in the ice with the ones in the floorboard. Not many people have such a memory of chucking fish out the window of a toasty-warm car, parked in the middle of a lake in 30-below January weather. That car always smelled like fish, oh, and marijuana.

Were all these nostalgic recollections just background scenery? Or, perhaps they were the play itself, pointing, no, screaming the most simple, most valuable message of all... live life, enjoy people, eat that delicious spaghetti in slow-motion, and go dancing for crying out loud. Having been raised in a very religious culture I spent most of my life dissecting and studying someone else's ancient translations of life rather than just living it out naturally. I know this now. And all the studying and digging and learning and devotion-based searching for significance ended up making a big, wide circle, eventually bringing me back around to the starting point... which is, like I said, simply living life in the here and now. Who would have thought that life really is just that simple?

One thing is certain for me at this point in my journey - forcing myself to view life only through the eyes of a few ancient religious writers - is no longer an option.

All this time the only thing needed was simply opening my eyes to the world I actually lived in, believing what observable reality clearly shows, and then living within those parameters and limitations... you know, "as if" the natural world we live in is enough. Having come from a religious background where not only nature was deemed to be not enough but me as well, this shift in thinking did not come easily or overnight.

Honesty is not the enemy

We can all be honest about what we ate last night, and we can usually come clean about the size of the fish we *almost* caught. Intelligent humans, as late as the sixteenth century, finally accepted that the sun doesn't orbit the earth. That was undoubtedly a difficult declaration for those who prided themselves in the *higher learning* of that era. Theologians to this very day are forced to make illustrious-sounding excuses and explanations for why two verses in the Old Testament, in plain point blank language, claim that the sun orbits our planet. There is also another verse clearly reporting that God once held the sun and the moon "in their place," stopping them from moving so a human military could kill more enemy combatants. The language in Joshua 10:13 about God "stopping" the actual movement of the sun and the moon (clearly showing that those ancient men believed in an orbiting sun) is so clear and cannot be spun (like theologians do) to say anything other than what it says... Are we ready to drop the whole ... "Well, God can do anything" excuse and really start thinking rationally about such things?

As difficult as this may be for some of the more biblical literalists to accept, planet earth p r o b a b l y didn't stop spinning for a few hours by the hand of some "God" so an ancient, regional military would have more light to kill by. Contrary to what we have heard from theological spin doctors, there are literally hundreds of blatant contradictions like this throughout the Bible. At one point in the book of Ezekiel, God is reported to have said of the city Tyre... "I will make you a bare rock, and you will become a place to spread fishnets. You will never be rebuilt, for I the LORD have spoken, declares the Sovereign LORD." And yet... Google maps shows that this city indeed *has* been rebuilt, and is a bustling commerce center with a beautiful marina... and probably a Starbucks.

It is not hard for people to concede that things like a talking snake, a rib woman, or a magical tree are almost certainly not to be taken literally, and a 1,500-mile CUBED golden city ("New Jerusalem") was obviously symbolic or metaphorical in nature, and not an actual city almost as large as our moon that will one day "land" on planet earth. No thinking person can walk away from the Sampson story of a man single-handedly killing 1,000 fully armed, fully battle trained soldiers and expert archers with a bone without at least a reasonable amount of skepticism. Millions have been convinced to accept some ancient narrative of all humanity having (literally) inherited some sort of voodoo-like ... curse, wherein we are all somehow infected on some unexplainable spiritual dna-level with a God-opposing nature, thus separated (in a legal sense) from a super-clean God — rendering us all as, well, not (legally) enough, not clean enough, not innocent enough, and therefore not acceptable enough for God. Although there are numerous ancient mythology-like Bible stories that we can all agree may just be legendary illustrations, allegories, or symbolic campfire *stories* with valuable lessons, some of the more foundational, fundamental doctrines were not to be questioned.

THE FOREST THROUGH THE TREES

Brutal, inner honesty...
The three scariest words on the planet,
and yet, at the same time,
the very KEY that unlocks all the doors...

Throughout the course of my life I have noticed that what real-life consistently revealed about the world I lived in was often in direct conflict with many of the things religion taught me. For the first half of my years here I just trusted that the theologians and scholars "must know what they are talking about." But somewhere between age 50 and 60 I began to ask myself, "What harm could possibly come from being brutally honest about what observable reality so clearly and so consistently shows us about the natural world we live in?" In many life-cases reality seems not only to *differ* from what religion teaches, but to nakedly showcase just the opposite.

In one of my previous books the subject of truth was discussed, and the conversation was one of contemplating the most accurate definition of truth. The best I could personally come up with was, "The way things really are here, and way things really work here." But how do things really work here? Throughout history very intelligent people have had to change their positions on many things they were at one point oh so certain of. As science and knowledge increased, so did the progress of abandoning many old world views and information that was eventually shown to be incomplete, incorrect, wrongly translated, or even mythological in nature. In this process we often find ourselves saying things like, "If those several things that have been taught so authoritatively for so many years are not literally true, then what *else* have I been taught that could also be untrue?"

This line of thinking makes a lot of people uncomfortable. In the minds of many, truth is what they have long-since decided it is, and much of that truth is based almost entirely on what they were told by people they trust. Also, much of what they were told was comforting, therefore quite easy not to question. Once their personal life experiences were explained and defined as "supporting evidence" for the ideologies they were being taught, an almost impenetrable wall was formed - of which even observable reality itself could not break through. It is for these that I write this unCOMFORTable book.

Truth is free, and it's also quite naked

This is the biggest lesson I've ever learned. Not only is truth completely free, but vividly out in the open... never was hidden in mystery or ancient writings that needed proper translations. Most of our studying and digging and searching into someone else's ancient religious writings has not been about finding or uncovering truth, but about hopefully finding comforting alternatives to truth, and then selling them to others until we finally believed them ourselves. For me personally, it has been a perpetual, never-completely-finding search for my own significance as a human. That is the heart and soul and reason for most theological study... to somehow, hopefully convince ourselves of our own value... that we are, well, okay. And so, I had become convinced by people I trusted that deeply studying the source literature that said I am not okay will somehow result in finally learning that I am. There's a solution for this, and it is called, "life, living, loving, and finally realizing that our hearts have always been much closer to the truth than our unfortunately-indoctrinated heads."

We are already significant, and always were. More importantly, we are enough, and always have been. All the answers we've ever needed have always been within us all this time... never hidden, never covered, never unseen. Many of us have literally been taught not to see this.

Two
"IF IT SOUNDS TOO GOOD TO BE TRUE…"

> *"One of the saddest lessons of history is this: If we've been bamboozled long enough, we tend to reject any evidence of the bamboozle. We're no longer interested in finding the truth. The bamboozle has captured us. It is simply too painful to acknowledge, even to ourselves, that we've been taken. Once you give a charlatan power over you, you almost never get it back."*
> *– Carl Sagan*

When "truth" is not true

It is somewhat easier to ignore obviously dark information than to dismiss mentoring that seems so full of comfort and encouragement. We have all had healthy and unhealthy mentors. And although certain negative influence is easy to spot, some information that is seemingly good-news is often also not true to tangible reality. When I was a young twenty-year-old just out of the military I remember a slobbering drunk at a local tavern sharing his *wisdom* with the younger crowd. Apparently, what he had *learned* from four failed marriages was that we should "treat a whore like a lady, and a lady like a whore." Around that same time I remember another man who drove an old beat-up pickup truck with the exhaust pipe held up with a coat hanger giving financial/business advice. His contention was that "it's not what you know, but who you know." Well, so much for higher education and a strong work ethic. The same person was also heard perpetually repeating the mantra of "the rich getting richer and the poor getting poorer…" But later on in life, having worked my way up into regional management in three different companies, I can confidently report that poverty is not always a simple broad-brush issue of inequality or unfairness from the more industrious, innovative crowd. We have all heard that republicans don't care about the children and that the democrats want you to lose your freedoms, both of which are obviously untrue.

We are all familiar with several of these more-than-obvious poor mentors. But what about teachings and ideologies which seem to be good, wholesome, and comforting - but are also untrue? Is there such a thing as good lies if they accomplish good things? You know… "little white lies"? In one of my earlier books I gave an analogy of an end-justifies-the-means example… If we dropped a thousand Bibles from an airplane on a few villages, the math alone would result in quite a few lives improving because of the valuable teachings of Jesus. But would that all be worth it if a single child got a broken neck from one of those hardcover books falling from the sky? Would that be a fair price to pay in order to "save" a village from unbelief? That's an extreme, hypothetical example, of course, but I really hope you never forget it. The end doesn't always justify the means.

Fact: Many people are walking around town with a very unhealthy self-image due to inherited religious beliefs about themselves that are simply not true - like the old Lowell Lundstrom song about once being so "wretched and poor," but now can finally sing, "Praise God, I'm a child of the King." Consequently, being a "child of the King" refers to one finally being accepted by God, in a very legal sense, legally-acquitted because of their faith - for the crime of (basically) being born a human.

"IF IT SOUNDS TOO GOOD TO BE TRUE..."

Imagine just for a moment
The real possibility
that most of what you've
been taught by religion
is not actually true to real-life reality.
How would you feel if you
suddenly learned that was the case?
What would that change?

"Got your dead rabbit and your dead raccoon..." – Bob Dylan

While walking through the forest with my dad as a child we chanced upon an incomplete collection of bones that once belonged to a small animal... perhaps a fox, or maybe a coyote. At one point those frail, decomposing bones had life surging through them, surrounded by muscle and ligament, as this now-completely-gone life form performed masterfully, spending its days frolicking in the sun-drenched woodland. "It's a part of life," my father said, pinching out the soft-burning embers at the end of his half-smoked cigarette. But if we chanced upon some human remains we probably wouldn't process it the same way. I still remember him gently pushing the bones around with the tip of his boot, saying something about a raccoon.

Growing up in a community of sportsmen, hunting and fishing was a major part of our culture. As a young person being raised with an evangelical background, many things in nature didn't make sense to me. Animals were seen basically as either walking meat factories or just pretty biological life forms for us to look at... you know, "designed" specifically for our viewing pleasure. All the thousands of mammals and millions of other "creatures" including insects and the microscopic world were "created" for a purpose by a wise "Creator," so we were told.

"And the only reason for honey
is for me to eat it."
- Pooh Bear

I once asked my dad why God made mosquitoes. Without hesitation he answered, "So the frogs can have something to eat." I then asked him why God made frogs. Again, a quick answer… "To keep the mosquito population down so we don't get carried away by them buggers." These answers were sufficient for a grade-schooler, but not for kid in junior high. I also remember asking him why God made bees, but as the word "bees" left my mouth I knew the answer would be – to make honey so we can eat it (which reminds me of Pooh Bear). "Okay," I thought to myself, "but wasps, hornets, and yellow jackets don't make honey…"

Not Dinotopia

In my last book a quite exhaustive conversation about the brutality of the dinosaur era was discussed. As a youngster it was hard for me to reconcile a loving, caring God who is all about goodness, beauty and kindness – creating the barbarous, indeed murderous realities of one dinosaur violently killing another who is shrieking in horror as the stronger one violently rips meat from its body. The church's "answer" for this obvious character-of-God dilemma was to blame the carnivore's behavior on, believe it or not, the "devil." The idea was sold that God created all animals as vegetarians, and then, when Adam disobeyed God, the mammal kingdom supposedly … switched from eating botanicals to killing each other for meat. Did someone just make all that up? Yes, they did. And yet there are those millions of years of incisor teeth with the obvious function of ripping meat. Hmmm. I was often given the Bible verse of the lion one day lying down with the lamb, as if this could perhaps be a reference to carnivores returning to their original diet of vegetables. This all sounded farfetched to me. How about you?

When you're an adolescent you pretty much accept whatever narrative your parents offer. But as you get older the really tough questions begin. Some of my main questions about animals were, "Do all animals go to heaven like us? Do they have souls? Why do the thousands of mammal species share an almost identical skeletal structure, internal organ system, and all of them, just like us, have two eyes, two ears, two nostrils, spinal cord, shoulders, elbows, wrists, hips, knees, ankles, feet, and reproductive system? Were the animals 'created in *our* image' and design, or did we indeed evolve from *their* even more ancient design?"

So many people like myself were taught the most fanciful things about the very natural world we live in. But all these ... almost fairy-tale-like interpretations of reality were always, well, hidden from plain view, and didn't seem to harmonize with nature or reality. I was beginning to see this as going way beyond convenient. What was not hidden is the observable reality of nature itself... the small collection of raccoon bones, the change of seasons, or the natural disaster being caused by earth's shifting tectonic plates. Nature was naked, vivid, and unmistakably clear to be exactly what it is. I thought to myself, "If there really is a God and some secret, magical kingdom, then wouldn't that God and all His stuff be right out in the open to be seen and understood just as vividly as nature is? Wouldn't it all be in perfect harmony with nature? And if not, then why not? My heart has always felt this way for some reason. I don't think I am alone. There is actually a verse in the New Testament section of the Christian Bible that says we should "come out into the light to be seen for what we are," and yet this (invisible) God I was taught about was obviously in perpetual hiding, and was also somehow conveniently excused from this same exhortation. Jesus once said we are to forgive each other 70 times 7, but God forgiving folks on that same level? Um... not so much. But if a God only accepts those who accept Him, how does that make Him better than us? I don't think this questioning is irreverent. I think its honest. And such honesty is not only unpopular in some circles, but discouraged. Why? No one wants to be questioned about personal beliefs that make no logical sense.

> *"Truth comes, but we can't hear it.*
> *How can we hear it, when we've been*
> *programmed to fear it?"*
>
> *- Lauryn Hill*

Adopted life translations

The essence of who we are was mystically defined by the church as "body, soul, and spirit," based on hopefully-accurate translations of several unrelated ancient Jewish verses. For instance, the Sadducees and the Pharisees had some major differences about life after death, but one of these groups sided with the beliefs of the even more ancient Egyptians on the matter. And now, to this very day, an enormous percentage of our population believes that we don't actually have to die in the same fashion as the poor, soulless raccoon. Quite unnaturally, they have been convinced that one of the main reasons they are here is to get safely to somewhere else. Raccoons, elephants, dolphins, and deer? Um... not so much, because "they don't have souls like we do," etc. But where oh where did who come up with what to make them decide this is factual knowledge? Can we be honest about this? At the very least, can we simply say out loud that we really don't know?

One day I just decided to start questioning several aspects of this whole ... need that some folks seem to have for animals to not have souls, or the need for animals to be on some significantly lower level of value as furry mammals than us. Then it suddenly hit me. If animals have souls (whatever souls are), then that would mean they also have the potential of "living forever," you know, like us, in some sort of animal heaven, if you will. If that's the case, then it would be a little harder for us to justify bleeding them out and cutting them into pieces to cook over fire. Perhaps this is why most religions view the animal kingdom, compared to us humans, as merely walking meat factories. I mean... just think about this for a few seconds. If humans are eternal, then why wouldn't other mammals also be? Someone might say, "But the animals kill each other for food." But wait a minute... so do we, to the actual extent of monolithic-sized, commercial slaughter houses – of which we don't like to think about. I guess since we are not gnawing raw flesh at their hind quarters as they are trying to escape that makes our form of killing "civilized." Don't get me wrong, I personally love a big, juicy cheeseburger, but I also no longer need to view the animal kingdom as lacking in some mystically-spiritual fashion. I had unknowingly inherited so many beliefs about such weird, unnatural things that I never really questioned. And I had never truly thought about it all. Until now...

> *"The most confused we ever get*
> *is when we try to convince our heads*
> *of something our hearts know is a lie."*
>
> *- Karen Moning*

"IF IT SOUNDS TOO GOOD TO BE TRUE..."

When I really started taking the effort and the honesty to examine what I absolutely knew compared to what I believed, I quickly found myself saying, "All is not right with some of the beliefs I have so lazily adopted as factual." So often, many of these inherited beliefs lacked even the slightest sliver of evidence, but I warmly embraced them as I was instructed. And again, it was easy for me because many of those beliefs were comfort-based. And there's a long list... everything from "the trinity" to a God who "loves" and "cares" for us in a similar fashion as a loving father or a best friend would. I was also taught about a universe that is (basically) at war with itself, i.e.: the natural world and "the spiritual world." This, of course, would have to mean that a God created nature, and then sort of as an afterthought – created SUPERnature as an even better alternative to the nature He first created and supposedly defined as "good." Sound ... confusing yet? Add to this list the possibility of somehow skirting around the dying process that all the other countless thousands of mammals, insects, and sea-going creatures must transition through. At one point I began to ask myself, "Are all these wild claims verifiable facts, or quite unverifiable, inherited, comfort-based beliefs?"

> *"I came across a fallen tree*
> *I felt the branches of it*
> *looking at me...*
> *Oh simple things,*
> *where have you gone?"*
> *- Kean*

Now in my early 60's I have found myself doing something I never had the courage to do earlier in life – sitting still on a downed tree in a quiet forest, thoughtfully contemplating the things in life that don't fit into the natural order of how things really are here. I think it is all about finally trusting our own hearts, our own logic, intuition, and deductive reasoning "as if" they were luxuries instead of enemies. I believe this same sort of introspection happens to many of us when we move into the autumn years of our lives. We finally begin to really see and accept what observable reality so vividly shows us... and always has been showing us. It is then that we also finally see how religion has defined what we are seeing as something quite different than what it is. Like some profound, but simple epiphany we begin to realize that many of the quite natural aspects of our existence have been defined and explained *for* us in a very mythological narrative construct, and that many of those explanations are not only contradictory to observable reality, but actually show themselves to be hopeful alternatives to some of the more uncomfortable realities of nature... death and dying being the main one.

Over the last couple of years while conversing with many different people from religion-based mindsets, it has become more than clear to me that many are often more interested in comfort than they are in truth. Personally, I reached a place in my journey where I had to finally admit that most of my religious beliefs really were about two main things... 1. Comfort, and 2. Fear of losing that comfort. Well, then there's #3, Judgment, which I felt gave me the license to judge who *had* the comfort and who *didn't* have the comfort. I don't know why I never saw this before, but I didn't, and perhaps because I couldn't.

As long as our God is a Judge
we too shall remain one.
And as one — the dream of ever
loving our neighbors "as ourselves"
remains absolutely impossible.

And no, it is not a God's job to
"love them through us."
That's OUR job.

Three
THE PREMISE VERSUS THE EVIDENCE

The Power of the Premise

The faith-based mentality of some…
"Since all the things the church taught us are 'true,' and beyond questioning, we just need to 'dig deeper into the Word' to solidly establish those inherited beliefs. If observable reality becomes a problem in this process, that too can be dealt with by simply believing our church denomination's translations of ancient scriptures rather than believing what real life vividly shows us. Because, remember… 'We don't live by sight (real life), we live by faith.' After all, what really is 'reality' anyway? Right?"

Does anyone actually take irrational that far? Although the above statement sounds, well… absurd, it is the process used by millions of people in their passionate attempts to protect, preserve, and maintain their inherited beliefs.

Honesty about harmony and consistency

The following quote is a vivid example of how the power of a strong premise is often not questioned… The late Thomas B. Warren, a professor at the Harding

School of Theology in Memphis, once said this, "Any method of interpretation is dangerous if it perverts the true meaning of scripture, and the ultimate test as to whether the true meaning of scripture has been ascertained, will be in the field of harmony and consistency. Any principle of interpretation that fails to advance harmony of thought and purpose in every related field of study must be considered as false. God's eternal purpose is so constituted and unfolded in the scriptures, and it is the only right method of interpretation that can be advanced entirely free of contradiction, inconsistency, or disharmony. The right method will not only meet the demands of the immediate scripture or context, but also of every related scripture or context."

If you'll please notice, Mr. Warren starts his quote with the inferred premise that his particular theological tribe is quite certain to have located the truest meanings of the scriptures (as does 40,000 other church denominations). Although he mentions the importance of "every related field of study," he also goes on to purport that the surest way to accurately secure truth is a matter of "harmony and consistency," not with the study of nature or reality or science or the real world we live in, but only with the other collections of ancient writings in the Bible itself. In this religion of the utmost faith that the Bible is a magical-propertied book that trumps even reality, "harmony and consistency" need not be in harmony or consistency with nature or even observable reality, but only with itself, its church-translated doctrines, and its writings. Many from this over-indoctrinated point of view, when confronted with reality not lining up with their Bible, become quite suspicious of reality rather than ever questioning "what the Bible says." In their sincerest belief - the Bible cannot be wrong or mistranslated in any way – because of its God-breathed, extraterrestrial status of being a quite magical book. I am personally alarmed at how many people still hold tightly to this ideal. Recently I suggested a few books on philosophy and theology to a religious fellow. He quickly replied, "Don't believe everything you read. I put my faith in God and His Word, not in the words of men!" But… wasn't the Bible actually written by men?

When I finally began to force myself into a more reasonable level of honesty about this, I had to admit to myself that it had actually been more important to me for my inherited doctrines to somehow synchronize with the Bible than with the real, out-here-on-the-ground world I lived in. Imagine being that fully indoctrinated without even knowing it. Like so many others, that was me. My supposedly-unquestionable, inherited Bible-based beliefs were "correct," mostly because I believed the translations I was given by the people I trusted.

This kind of honesty did not come easy for me. I don't think it comes easy for anyone from my evangelical background to finally admit such things.

Honesty about the foundational stuff

For the last forty years I have watched and listened to so many church doctrines being revised, changed around, reformatted, new terminology added, and hopefully retranslated into more accurate interpretations. I would give the long list of significant doctrines most churches have revised over the last four decades but I've already covered that in other books. Most parishioners didn't have too many problems with all those upgraded doctrines, and for two main reasons... 1; the changes, even the drastic ones, were introduced very gently and over a period of time, so most people never even noticed the changes. And 2; because their main two or three foundational beliefs were not among the list of changeable doctrines. And what are those two or three?

1. There is a God-Person, and He loves and cares about me.
2. He answers my prayers and is always taking care of me.
3. Adherent, devotional belief in His son makes me eligible for heaven.

There may be a couple more untouchables, but those are the main three. Whether or not Jesus is ever physically coming back here can be respectfully debated between the futurist and preterist positions of eschatology with the host of Christian scholars in both of those groups. Is heaven a real, physical place or some beyond-explanation intergalactic, unseen dimension? It doesn't matter. Do angels have wings? It doesn't matter. Is the pastor's interpretation of grace doctrinally sound? It doesn't matter. Is tithing a requirement or a principle or belongs exclusively with someone else's ancient Middle Eastern religion? It doesn't matter. Was the apostle Paul really basing his view of women on Eve being from Adam's rib? Was the Noah's ark story a regional or global flood or an even more ancient legend? It matters not. Was the ascension about Jesus disappearing into the foggy hills, or did he actually float up into the stratosphere? Is there an actual "devil"? These things do not matter to most of the folks from the evangelical camp I came from. The pastor or denomination can restructure their translations of grace, eschatology, and even reinterpret the meaning and function of the crucifixion story itself (as the grace movement has recently done). Many of my readers have seen this over the course of their lives in the church. But what they haven't seen is a serious, honesty-based questioning of the big three. And what do the big three all have in common? Comfort, comfort, and ... comfort...

1. God loves me like a Daddy
2. Takes care of me
3. I never have to die

Their "reality" became our "reality"

These are beliefs we have all been taught as facts, along with the support of Bible verses we have all been authoritatively assured are "evidence." But are religious passages of stories that were told around ancient desert campfires really evidence? Not only were these things taught to us as unquestionable facts, but many of our very real personal life experiences have also been explained and translated *for* us by the church. When this is done to us at an early age from such an authoritative platform, in our minds those explanations become "the truth" to us. They become "the real world." Here's an example... If things were going exceptionally well, then God was really blessing me that week. But if my world suddenly took a nose dive, as life sometimes does, then either the devil was attacking me or God was trying to teach me something. That, of course, is an oversimplified analogy, but in many ways an accurate one. The point is that I had trustingly adopted many incontestable premises from other people, both modern-day as well as ancient. The second part is that for so long I was often in an odd but blatant sort of denial about this. And I've been bumping into an increasing number of people from my background who are now also sharing the same honesty.

My friend and fellow author Joshua Tongol recently said that we all process our personal experiences, both big and small, through the grid of belief systems we were given. Like my friend Joshua's story - I also used a much different standard when critiquing *other* religions about *their* beliefs that sounded absurd. But because I had long-since accepted my inherited religion as basically faultless, any of *our* beliefs that sounded unrealistic were immediately excused with any number of "explanations" or guesses offered by the clergy. Worst-case scenario — we would just say, "God's ways are higher than ours," or ... "We just have to trust and believe what the Bible says, and not question such things..."

I believe if people mustered up enough honesty they could probably count on one hand the number of things they have learned experientially which led to forming their philosophy, and then be able to admit that most of the other "ten thousand things" were teachings they blindly adopted as "truth" from people they admired. Yes, all of us.

Honesty about our experiences

I don't judge other people's experiences, because experiences are very real. What I am starting to seriously question now is all the definitions, explanations, and translations *of* those real experiences. But experiences are not "evidence" of correct doctrines, they are evidence of experiences.

> *"Experience is what we get when we don't get what we want.*
> *And it is often the most valuable thing we have to offer."*
>
> *- Randy Pausch*

There actually could be more accurate-to-reality explanations than the mythology-like narratives we've been given, many of which we have yet to even consider. Obviously, everyone must do their own questioning, their own doubting, their own research, their own believing, and then come to their own personal conclusions. It would be one thing if beliefs were all we inherited, but even more important, and more powerful than beliefs, are the religion-based explanations and definitions we have been given for the very real life experiences we have. Everything from our own mental contemplations to bumping into our friend Sharon at the shopping mall has been defined as a "God" moving the pieces. Yes, even our own thoughts have been defined as "God speaking to us." Or, if we happen to allow our thinking to drift over into more low energy thinking, then "the devil" (not us) is trying to distract us from the good things of God in the hopes of bringing us down. And so on the one hand we were taught to be careful not to take ownership of our good thoughts, lest we become prideful. And on the other hand we didn't have to take full responsibility for all of our bad thoughts because we could blame "the enemy" of our souls for that. Honestly? This is not a recipe for long-term, sustainable personal growth *or* maturity. Is this not a philosophy of denial of what is? And what do we do when we don't get what we want from God? Well, if we want to keep our beliefs of a loving, caring, comforting, protecting God alive – we must do whatever it takes, including making up spiritual-sounding reasons for God's lack of response or performance.

Some of the very foundational tenets of the religion I was raised with sharply contradicted nature and observable reality. What's worse is that the actual bulk of the evidence seemed to be leaning heavily in the more naturalist camp, not in the foundational teachings I received as a child. If such a statement can be clearly demonstrated to be true, what would we do with that? How would we process that? Will we have the courage to accept what observable reality actually shows on these subjects, or would we muster up some desperate, emotion-based loyalty to the doctrinal paradigms from an older generation of predecessors? Would we try to explain away the evidence, or would we be brave enough to finally agree that some of the things we were taught simply *don't* add up? Well, let's see…

Honesty about God's character sketch and the Job Complex

If we truly examine the benevolent, all-caring Santa-like "God" the church has sold us we will most likely recall a character sketch of a "loving heavenly

Father" Who really "cares" about us, and is "closer than any brother," but, is also a Judge. And yet if we really inspect what every day ordinary life shows we get a much different picture. We can certainly make all sorts of romantic-sounding excuses for these blatantly obvious discrepancies, but we can't make them go away...

I'd like to start this by awakening my readers to the fact that an exponentially-growing group of people are now viewing "God" as more of an explanation than an actual anthropomorphic, Santa-Claus-like invisible Entity out-there-somewhere in the ethers. In my book, *What Is God, And How Does It Work*, we discussed at length the history of "God." Ancient men from every culture, in their sincere attempts to explain and define their very real interactions with the operational mysteries of the universe, began to construct a Supreme ... "Person" that was, in so many ways, very much like themselves. One only needs to read the Bible from cover to cover to realize this.

Most people, even atheists, acknowledge some sort of ... organic "intelligence" that permeates all of nature, and that some type of Life Force System indeed controls and maintains the operational dynamics of our world. At this point in our scientific "understanding" of the universe, there is unarguably both order and patterns that, in my opinion, point to a definite "operating system" of sorts that governs every atom in every corner of 500 billion galaxies. I will be the first person to admit that I simply don't have all the answers of how it all actually works. But I will also be one of the first people to step up and confidently say, "It most certainly is not a GUY with human characteristics and demeanors." We could walk and talk about this for hours on a good stretch of beach. My first two books already cover this subject at great length. However, what we will do today is showcase a vivid comparison between what religion teaches and what observable reality shows. Here we go...

"Closer than a brother"

The other day I read an article from a preacher, stating, "There is a friend that is closer than a brother." The young pastor was referring, of course, to either God,

Jesus, or both. And yet if an *actual* brother knew that his sibling was lost in the forest without food or water, with the bitter-cold night closing in, and knew the location of this starving, thirsting brother, he would go quickly to his side with food, water, and directions out of the forest. The church's explanation for why the biblical God (who is supposedly closer than the actual brother) will stand by and let the man die alone in the forest is what I call "The Job Complex." The Old Testament story of a person named Job begins with an introduction to Job's character. He is described as a blessed man who lived righteously in the Land of Uz. God's praise of Job prompted the devil to challenge Job's integrity, suggesting that Job served God simply because God protected and blessed him. So God takes the challenge from Satan and removes His protection, allowing the evil one to take Job's wealth, kill his children, and even take his physical health in order to test Job's character and devotion to God. But despite his broken state of grief and desolation he did not curse God. And although he anguished intensely, he stopped short of ever accusing God of injustice. And this is where the all-too-familiar quote comes from, "Though he slay me, yet I will hope and trust in Him..." I don't know about you, but to me – trusting someone who is trying to slay me, or is gladly allowing someone else to slay me – is not my idea of a good King or a good God.

Job's story has been used by many a theologian and parishioner alike to hopefully somehow explain why God would not act like someone who actually is closer than a real brother. Some of the explanations are as follows… "Perhaps God had a reason for allowing the lost hunter to die that is much deeper than we can comprehend." Or… "Maybe the infinite, all-knowing God allows things like this to happen for reasons us mere finite mortals could never understand." Or… "Perhaps the disoriented sportsman simply didn't have the proper amount of faith in his desperate prayers for God's help." Or… "Could it be that God wants us to find our own way out of the forest to maybe … teach us something about trusting Him more?"

Unfortunately, what all of these guesses do not contain is the absolute brutal honesty that this "God of the Bible" ISN'T actually closer than a brother, nor does such a "He" care about us in any way similar to how a real-life sibling or father does. This is why, in my second book, I describe God as "Perfectly-Impersonal" and "Wondrously-Indifferent." Why? Because that is what century upon century upon century of observable reality so very clearly shows us. And so, it would appear that observable reality isn't the problem, our willingness to be completely honest about it is.

Abba Father / Papa / Daddy

The reason we want there to be a Daddy is because we were taught to want and need one. In truth, my Daddy had the same last name as me… You know, the same guy who worked the long hours, bought the groceries, and changed my diapers.

Nevertheless, the church has given us a "loving and caring (heavenly) Father." I have heard many people actually refer to "Him" affectionately as "Papa" or "Daddy." Is this … romantic? Absolutely. Does it bring comfort to millions of people? Yes. Just a day or two ago I chanced upon a contemporary Christian song on the radio where the musical group was singing in devotional style, "Oh how He loves us. Oh how He loves us…" But is this accurate to reality? Do we have any concrete proof of this love? Well… visible to this very day, carved into the wall in one of the crude, animal-stall-like barracks at Auschwitz in Poland are the words, "If there is a God, He will have to beg my forgiveness." If we can be truthful, we do not have real answers for this. What we have, if we are honest, are guesses. And the reason we have had to guess about things like this is because our beliefs didn't match up with reality.

With our actions we say, "Something has to be done." And that something is the methodical, awkward explaining away of observable reality and the lack of evidence for the romantically-embraced beliefs of our predecessors. Meanwhile, the woman who is "walking in covenant with the Lord" gets the same incurable cancer as the atheist does. So much for the "I will if you will" law of reciprocity. Who among us is arrogant enough to tell the Auschwitz prisoner or the cancer patient that they simply didn't "fully understand" the love of God?

A few months ago while listening to a Christian music station for research on this book, a man called into the radio station… He tells the radio announcer how horribly guilty he feels for placing his wife and children in a higher priority level than his time alone with God in prayer. The radio announcer, acting like a spiritual guide, commended the poor fellow for wanting to get his time-management priorities straight, and even prayed a prayer with him, asking God to forgive him. My take on this? Unhealthy insanity!

There seems to be a widely-shared dysfunctional view of the man Jesus among many theists, having been convinced by preachers and theologians that all his words were intended for a global, timeless audience. Couple that with the teaching that he was also the Creator of the universe, and you get all sorts of fear-based devotion that, in all honesty, is way beyond irrational in nature, not to mention exegetically incorrect. And so, several personal conversations Jesus was having with his closest first-century friends led to stuff like the following…

A sincere woman, speaking fondly of her precious granddaughter, said this… "Nothing in the world except Jesus beats a granddaughter." (Probably "inspired" by the conversation Jesus was having with his friends in Matthew 10:37, "He who loves father or mother more than Me is not worthy of Me; and he who loves son or daughter more than Me is not worthy of Me.") For someone in twenty-first-century Atlanta, Georgia to take that literally is not only incorrect in my view, but unhealthy and unrealistic.

A man recently told me, "God is not my religion. God is someone I study. God is not somewhere out in the distance. God is my Abba Daddy. God is my friend whom I walk with in this life and in the next. God is my closest relative." (#1, imagine "studying" your wife. #2, If the Creator of 500 billion galaxies is your "friend" who you walk with, then you walk with an "invisible friend." And I guess that's okay, if you can admit that, but, #3, in my personal opinion, when invisible friends become closer than your own spouse and your own children or grandchildren, there is something wrong. Truthfully, no such loyalty has EVER been required of us by Jesus or a God.)

There was a devout theist who engaged in a conversation with me about a loving heavenly Father. After I listed several heartbreaking examples of how his God supposedly stands idly by and watches, or … "allows" horrendous suffering, from everything to natural disasters to crying, praying parents losing a child to cancer, I asked him an important question, also requesting that he really try to be brutally honest about the answer… The question was… "Do you think your God loves and cares about your wife and children more than you do?" His answer was quick and needed no thought... "Of course God loves them more than I do, and more than I ever could." He replied. When I asked him to give me just a couple of real-life examples of his God loving and caring for people more than humans do, the conversation fell immediately silent... just the sound of evening crickets. This was ... alarming to me, and I understood just how strong the whole *Job Complex* indoctrination could actually be. He spoke with great conviction, just like a good and faithful believer does, but of "truths" that he had absolutely no evidence for in the real world we live in. That's why they call it "belief."

The caring God Who doesn't (really) care

Perhaps I am in good company with the concentration camp prisoner... A Christian friend of mine recently suggested that my commentary on this subject is "lacking in the deeper understandings of God." I quickly replied, "I may not understand all the deeper understandings of God, but what I am not lacking in is observation." He replied with yet another devotion-based guess... "God is not a Father or brother in the same exact sense as physical brothers and fathers are. But God is our Father nonetheless." I thought to myself, "How convenient is that? We can romantically paint God as an Entity who loves and cares about us, and is closer than any brother, but when real-life situations vividly show that this is not the case – we can employ the Job Complex or any number of acceptable, church-sanctioned guesses. And so... if a child gets abducted, raped, and killed, an all-caring, all-knowing, all-powerful, loving, protective "Father" who is "closer than a brother" can be completely excused for not caring, not loving, not protecting, and not showing any traits of actually being closer than a brother. And there are so many different ... illustrious-sounding theories from the scholarly crowd of theologians who will tell us things about free will, a God who doesn't medal with our lesson-learning human experiences, and, believe it or not – the outlandish claim that God "perhaps" allows suffering for our character development. And this is where we finally realize that some preachers, perhaps unknowingly, are actually teaching that God (literally) created suffering as a sort of ... gift for us, you know... to help us grow, etc. Is this not irrational? No?

Recently, a girl named Cathy shared a grace preacher's video sermon on the love of God, but prefaced it with the words, ""Oh God, please help us to see how much you love us!"

HONEST QUESTION: If I sat idly by and watched your child drown in an ice-cold river, would you say that I "must have had my valid reasons" for not intervening, and then ask ME to be your family's grief counselor? Honest question... Do you think you could ever be talked into such irrational behavior in your state of grief? I realize that these kinds of honest discussions really injure some people, but please try to remember - this is a book about honesty. My simple goal is the truth about reality, not hopeful alternatives for the truths that are a bit too uneasy for us to admit or talk about.

"Mad, angry, hurt, wounded, or lost..."

Some make the mistake of supposing that I am either angry or perhaps "mad at God" for some unfortunate event in my past. On the contrary, I am completely okay for there not even being an actual God/Person/Entity at all, and am very much at peace with this possibility, and such a full level of personal responsibility for my own life. It doesn't scare me, not in the least, nor does it leave me lonely or without meaning and purpose.

Is my honesty too brutal? Should we not question such things? Should we not publicly acknowledge observable reality for what it shows itself to be? Is that us? Are we ... afraid that reality could actually be "truth"? Must someone have hate or bitterness in their hearts towards Christianity if they openly question these foundational beliefs? Really? Is that really how we paint genuine truth seekers? This rationale is where some folks go when they can't bear to listen honestly to conversations like this. Logic goes out the window, and emotion takes over... And then we hear things like, "This writer is attacking my faith and trampling on the Holy Word of God!" A friend named Larry told me, "Ken, your perceptions are skewed from the bitterness you have related to your own experiences. A person doesn't have to deny everything he once knew to be true for the sake of launching out on a mission to discredit Christianity." I of course explained to my friend that I have no bitterness in my heart for Christianity or for the church, but simply no longer view many of the beliefs I once thought were true as true anymore.

Another person asked me, "Ken, why do you need to change anyone? How about just loving them for where they are?" Well, the clergy had the only microphones for several decades... a very powerful place of dogmatic authority to be. But now, because of social media – EVERYONE has a microphone. A very valued mentor named Clarence from my home town once said, "Ken, I love people right where they are, but too much to leave them that way." I guess that would be my answer to this person as well. When you have finally found the real freedom and inner peace you've been searching for your entire life, you just want to take as many people with you as possible. It's called sharing and caring.

Another person, a passionate Methodist, said this... "Ken, freedom for what? To finally break out of a cage is indeed refreshing and liberating, but then what? Is it now your life purpose to keep returning to fight the cage? If so, it would seem that you've hardly broken free. Are you like bodhisattva, motivated by love to return over and over to set others free?"

I guess my answer to that is that there is plenty of "shaking" going on... I shake the cage, and then I get the shake down for shaking it. This comes as no surprise to me. But let me make something very clear... "You" are not "the cage." So one doesn't "fight the cage," one simply exposes the cage for what it is. And then, those who want to leave do precisely that.

"Not Exactly Like..."

If God is "not exactly like a regular father," and "not exactly like a real brother," then why on earth would we continue promoting this God as such? Because "the Bible (and pastor) tells us so." This is a most interesting revelation, wherein believers completely accept a concept that not only has no proof, but where the irrefutable evidence of just the opposite is abundant, and on a global scale. This is what so much of biblical apologetics is about... biased, indoctrinated scholars coming up with all sorts of lofty-sounding scenarios (guesses) to explain away the obvious. Do we want to talk about this? No, we most certainly do not, nor do we want to even think about it. Because if we investigate too fully, too deeply – we may end up having to totally rethink a bunch of what we currently believe.

The other day I saw an illustration of a man walking aimlessly through an expansive, brick wall maze... entitled, FAITH is trusting God even when you don't understand His plan." But if that is their definition of faith, then pray tell – what is their definition of REASON? Is reason the enemy of faith? If so, why would that make any logical sense?

A man in his mid-60's told me the other day, "If I ever lost my wife I would never remarry." His reason was that it would be like starting all over again... A very similar position is taken by many who begin to realize that much of their hand-me-down theology is probably not correct. The mindset... "I'd have to start all over again, and I don't want to have to do that."

Four
THE JOB STORY COMPLEX

Honesty about Contemporary Christian music

When channel surfing the FM stations on my morning commute I chanced upon a Christian music station. Here are just a couple of (very telling) song lyrics I ran across...

Song #1

(The singer talking to God...)
When You don't move the mountains I'm needing You to move
When You don't part the waters I wish I could walk through
When You don't give the answers as I cry out to You
I will trust, I will trust, I will trust in You!

I was sure by now God You would have reached down
And wiped our tears away
Stepped in and saved the day

But once again, I say "Amen," and it's still raining
As the thunder rolls I barely hear Your whisper through the rain
"I'm with you"
And as Your mercy falls I raise my hands
and praise the God who gives
And takes away
[Chorus:] And I'll praise You in this storm
And I will lift my hands
For You are who You are
No matter where I am
And every tear I've cried
You hold in Your hand
You never left my side
And though my heart is torn
I will praise You in this storm

 But does anyone really "hear the voice of God whispering through the rain," or witness His "mercy falling down upon us"? Does a God "hold our tears in His hands"? Is this not all more like romantic, hopeful poetry than actual reality? I believe these to be honest questions that can actually lead to a more liberating and empowering personal growth and wellness. After all, isn't that what truth does best? Truth has always set us free from the things that are not true. And isn't that what we all really want?

Song #2

Another heartbreak day
Feels like you're miles away
Don't even need no shade
When your sun don't shine
Too many passin' dreams
Roll by like limousines

It's hard to keep believin'
When they pass you by and by
I know your heart has been broke again
I know your prayers ain't been answered yet
I know you're feeling like you got nothing left
Well, lift your head, it ain't over yet, ain't over yet

Those lyrics actually remind me of the Pink Floyd song with the words, "Hanging on in quiet desperation is the English way…" Is this not just another example of someone attempting to excuse God for not acting like God? Can we be honest? In a sentence – Someone is having a bad day and they want some mystical, doctrine-based reasons for it.

More…

In the middle of the night
When worry finds me
In the middle of the fight
When strength is gone
In the middle of a fire
When fear is closing in
You are, You are my song
You're my hope, when hope is gone

I will cast my cares on You the Almighty
I will cast my cares on You 'cause You're good
I will cast my cares on You 'cause You love me, You love me
Oh, oh because You love me

You were reaching through the storm
Walking on the water
Even when I could not see

HONESTY: THE FINAL FRONTIER

In the middle of it all
When I thought You were a thousand miles away
Not for a moment did You forsake me

The song writer sings, "When I thought You were a thousand miles away…" But why would he think that? Is it because that is (honestly) how he feels? And why would it feel like that? Is it even possible that he could be mistaking intuition with feelings? From all my years in the church I can definitely relate to how easy it is to confuse the two, especially when we were warned about the "danger" of using our hearts as truth detectors. Not only was I told what to feel, but how to feel about it. And what of the beliefs that make us feel less than we really are?

Here's a song by Carrollton called "Tell me"…

Feel like I'm a nobody
Wonder if I'll ever amount to much
Seems like no matter what I do
It's never gonna be good enough
Should I just give up?
Lord, I need to hear You speak

(Please keep in mind that this is being written and sung by someone who is in the church and repeatedly says they believe that God is always with them and in them…) But if that's so, then why all the insecurity?

Tell me I am loved
Tell me I am known
That You died for me
I am not alone
Tell me I'm Your child
The one Your heart beats for
I can find my strength
Knowing I am yours

You've always known what my heart needs
And You tell me

You tell me I am loved
You tell me I'm Your child
Lord, You tell me
Oh, You tell me

    If we are honest, what we see here is a person who has been told that their value and significance lies *outside* of themselves in the (taught) need of being accepted and loved by some Supreme Being. It is more than interesting how the singer here is basically asking God to please confirm all the things his pastor has taught him. But why all the uncertainty? Could it be because his heart somehow knows something is wrong? And although the singer talks of hearing this Entity "tell him" that he is loved and accepted and valued, there really is no such extraterrestrial voice telling him any such thing. Rather, he is chanting in devotional fashion what he has been told is true. Yes, he is talking to HIMSELF and pretending that his own thoughts are a God talking to him. Can we really not see this and acknowledge our own honesty about this? In fact, many cannot. Many people believe what they do because there is maternal-like comfort in it. In short, if we are honest, contemplation, meditation, self-introspection, and conclusion formulation is not "the voice of God."

    Talking to ourselves and working things out in our minds, or blissful, thoughtful, insightful moments is not a God talking to us, but natural human attributes we all share, including law-of-attraction abilities that we are just now beginning to scratch the surface on understanding. But if all our personal epiphanies were defined for us as something a God is doing or imparting – it is understandable how we would eventually also believe and adopt such things.

    Are we really "hearing from God," or are we hearing from our own thoughts, intuition, and connectedness to each other and the universe that birthed us? Having conversations/contemplations with yourself is perfectly normal, right up to the point of (unknowingly) calling yourself "God," claiming that you are "hearing from God." That's where you lose me.

"Same as it ever was, same as it ever was…"

And you may ask yourself… why these depressing song lyrics never change decade after decade after decade… and why so many Christians, like these song writers, seem to be in an unending, emotion-based … battle field where they never progress beyond this ultra-dependent mentality. I personally know people who have completely conquered their depression, low self-image, and even overcame extremely traumatic life events through professional counseling and even simply from reading a few self-help books. But that's a whole other conversation about taking 100 percent personal responsibility for our own happiness, our own demeanor, and our own personal growth and mental wellness. I hate to be the one to say it, but religion teaches just the opposite… that you can't improve yourself on your own behalf – because you really aren't that amazing… you really aren't that strong… you really aren't that intelligent or innovative or able to process good information into new ways of thinking and being. And in some church circles it's even worse, because they tell people that they are helpless without a God assisting them so they can get through the week without falling apart.

What I am hearing in all these lyrics is 1; normal everyday life can include bad days and challenging times, and 2; these singer's desperate attempts to have some sort of deeper/spiritual meanings or reasons for it other than just simple, everyday life challenges. But the only true reason is nature. Nature, real life is not always easy and fun, period. But we help each other through the hard times and celebrate with one another in the good times. We, us, *real* people… *real* brothers and *real* sisters and *real* fathers and *real* mothers and *real* friends… WE are the ones who do the (actual) loving and caring and comforting of each other. Please ask yourself if you really think a God loves and cares for your children and spouse more than you do. I think our hearts already know the answer to that question. If not, what does observable reality tell us?

Comfort's Origins

If our comfort in time of need (actually) comes from God, then why would we even need people to tell us or remind us in our time of need that it does? The comfort would automatically be there and very recognizable to us as being from God. Or is religion-based comfort just "comforting things we tell ourselves about a God" to, you know... comfort ourselves? If God is real and He ... "comforts us," then why would this God hide so stealthfully – to the extent of even the strongest, most devoted believer, after decades of service still find themselves in such insecure, unsure states as to have to ask God things like, "Oh Lord, please show me that You're there, that You love me, and that I'm not alone!"? Why would we need to be shown *anything* after 40 years of a relationship with someone? In reality, we wouldn't. But we do, and there's a reason for it... our inner voice of honesty. God doesn't do what they said He does, nor is "He" what they say He is.

These are very telling questions, aren't they? Doesn't our comfort actually come from the people in our lives? Isn't it really them who step up and "comfort us"? Are they really being "used" by a God to comfort us? That sounds just a bit ... demeaning and dismissive of the people who actually come to our aid, doesn't it? Is their own humanitarian love not quite enough to get the comforting job done for us? Why minimize the love and care and benevolent acts of our family and friends by giving the credit to some invisible Entity for what *they* did? Can we really not see this? No?

Where My Comfort Comes From

My comfort does not come from doctrine-based theology, belief systems, life philosophies, or invisible cosmic Beings. I get freedom and knowledge and potential from my own study of life and personal life experiences, but all my comfort (all of it) comes from other people and myself. I use my own human attributes to troubleshoot, brainstorm, consciously employ recollection of what has worked for me and others in the past, self-talk, intention and resolve to make good choices - while entertaining, cultivating, and nurturing healthy thinking. Although I may find physical comfort in a blanket, a warm fire, or even a crude bed of straw, all my encouragement, inspiration, comradery, social and emotional comfort come from other people and from myself taking 100 percent responsibility for my own well-being.

A girl named Jennifer said, "There are so many times where I don't feel the comfort of others and that is when I seem to watch my mind imagine a loving 'God' who does. Sometimes it helps because that is really what I am looking for... comfort. However I have to be honest and say I question the existence of such an Entity all the time."

A person named Dee said, "When you look objectively it is the people around us that bring us comfort and love in times of need. I think the whole "God is our comfort" thing is a bit of a cop out from people that find the idea of being our ongoing support and comfort daunting. Maybe because of them not knowing who they truly are themselves and being comfortable in their own skin. I think mainline Christianity with its performance focus has influenced this. It's all part of the religious deconstruction that many of us are going through. It's like wisdom... Wisdom doesn't just drop from the sky, knowledge and understanding are needed, and mostly this comes from living life over the years and accumulating it consciously and subliminally. Then one day you start getting the real aha moments, and as you pay attention - the wisdom comes. It's not an 'out there' coming in, it's an 'in there' coming out."

In a contemporary Christian song called, "Redeemed" (by Big Daddy Weave) the singer says, "All of my life I have been called unworthy, named by the voice of my shame and regret..."

And yet what is the one life philosophy that teaches that we are unworthy, shameful, and regretful? Is it not the very religion the singer represents? I can't help from thinking about that old verse, "Who TOLD you that you were naked?" The answer? The pastor did. The very title of the song, "Redeemed," is a word that describes what is known among Bible scholars as penal substitution... and the very definition of the word is to "buy back"... in other words someone (Jesus) paying God the price He demanded (a torturous murder) in order for us to finally be rendered as "enough" for Him... acceptable enough, clean enough, good enough, eligible enough, and forgiven enough. Are we ready to have an intelligent, adult conversation about this?

*"You're needy, ugly, and helpless, but we can help,"
said the salesman holding the big bag with the words,
"low-self-esteem" and "you're not enough" written on it...*

As a child I never even thought about the concept of "freedom." It had not yet become a need. The "need" had to be taught to me. Think about that... Did someone say, "Stockholm syndrome"? Please try to wrap your head around the same company that sold you cigarettes now selling you nicotine patches. Very similar story.

The 'Hidden Message' in Christian Music

(From *Field of Grasshoppers*)

> For a project of my own, I listened to a Seattle-based contemporary Christian radio station for only two daily commutes. The main themes in most of the music I heard was about:

1. How terribly hard, almost unbearable, it is 'down here below' in this burdensome world...
2. An almost begging, ultra-dependent neediness and crying to 'God up above' to please 'come down' and help us through our day, week, month, year, and life. To me, this seems so contradictory to what many Christians often boldly declare about "Christ in us" and Immanuel (God with us) and "Lo, I am always with you" and "We are the salt of the earth and the light of the world."
3. An emotion-based romance, almost lamenting for some future utopian, off-planet paradise that will be so much better than the life we have to struggle through here in the here and now.

> The clear, underlying message in the music revealed a completely different people whose God is very much still 'up there,' or out there somewhere, separate from them, and they of course, 'down here below.'

Here are just a few statements from the songs I quickly jotted down as I was driving:

- Come down, Oh Lord...
- Shine down on us...
- I'm trusting that God knows what He's doing in my life...
- I can't do this on my own...
- Here I am at the door, praying that You'll let me back in...
- I can focus on the score, but I can never win...
- I'm not strong enough to be what I'm supposed to be...
- This world has nothing for me, this life is not my own...
- I can't trust myself to do what's right...
- I am stained with dirt, prone to gravity...
- Help me find Your will...
- My soul is crushed from the weight of this world...
- Let me know the struggle ends...
- I'm all alone, with the night closing in on me...
- Throw me a lifeline and rescue me...
- God, I need You now...
- When I feel like giving up...
- Without You I fall apart...
- Lord, pull me out of this mess I'm in...
- Lord I know that I've let You down...
- My heart is heavy from what it takes to keep on breathing...
- I was sure by now that You would have reached down...
- When my strength is gone, and I can't carry on...
- When I'm in the storm, under the weight of the world...
- Let me see through Your eyes...
- Oh Lord, I can't hardly breathe without You...
- Please help me to please You more...
- God, please be near...

Here's the irony in all of this; The fifties crowd in the church have abandoned the old hymns, claiming (rightfully) that they were full of incorrect and often depressing doctrines of an earlier generation. Yet this 'contemporary' music is doing the same exact thing, perpetually crying out in helpless desperation to an Entity that is still viewed as being very much separate from us. This continual barrage of sad, desperate dependency actually fosters an emotional, soap opera-like, daily lifestyle. Why would I want that? And so, "Whatsoever things are ... think on these things" becomes "Oh, God, please help us make it through the week!" Meanwhile the 'non-Christian' gang is 'making it through the week' just fine.

The radio station's 'top of the hour' jingle statement? "Hope and Encouragement in these Troubled Times." But wait a minute: I'm not troubled. Am I supposed to be troubled? One woman called in and made a statement of which the radio station (actually) saved as something to use repeatedly for their advertisement promo. Here it is, and I quote: "If I am not listening to your radio station at work, I don't have peace." I sincerely wish I were making this stuff up.

I began to realize that it is not the lyrics of these songs that are 'all wrong,' it is the theology. It is the theology that is creating this perpetual ultra-dependency that never progresses beyond a certain point. I have a funny feeling that many of my readers can relate to my conclusions. Even though some of the music styles try to emulate the newer, secular music sounds, it stays seemingly imprisoned within the pop, 'bubble gum' status that still evokes toe tapping from even the oldest pastor. It is just 'progressive' enough to make the Christian music buyer feel that their music is indeed 'contemporary.' Completely unknown to most Christian music lovers, those outside the church see most of it as a religious-driven alternative to quality music.

The Strange Romance for Anywhere Else (But Here)

In some of the songs, there seemed to be a continual psychological love affair for some distant place that is "Oh, so much better than Earth," which sadly creates a strange sort of contempt for the natural world of the here and now. This *boredom* and irreverence for the world we are in is strange at best. It is almost as if they wish death would come faster so they could get out of this nasty, horrible place God supposedly called 'good.' One day when God "calls our name" we will "rise on eagle's wings" and finally get to where we really want to be, because "this world is not our home," etc. Can someone please explain to me the romantically euphoric anticipation of one day physically seeing Jesus face-to-face? What on earth is that about? One of the songs I heard was an anthem of wanting to finally be away from this cruel world and be in heaven entitled, "I Can Only Imagine."

But why not imagine the amazing connectedness we already have with both "God" and our fellow man, right here, right now? Why not imagine a great picnic day at the beach with family, good friends, good food, and fellowship? Why not imagine how you are going to change the world and heal the world and make a difference on a practical level? Why not imagine growing into adulthood, where people eventually grow out of their religiously inherited, soap opera-like, emotional illnesses, becoming all they were meant to become here? Why not stop trying to be a 'good Christian' (as if we owe that to someone), and just focus on becoming a mentally and intellectually and philosophically stable and healthy and happy professional human being?

Another song that stuck in my mind as odd was of a congregation chanting the words: "Take this world and give me Jesus. This is not where I belong." Excuse me? The planet you were born on is not where you belong? First of all, when people die here, it is not because 'God called their name,' it is because they died. Secondly, why would we want to leave the place where God supposedly placed us? Just recently I watched a preacher pray (and I quote) "Jesus, I'm a stranger in this world, and I don't belong here. You will soon be coming to take me home to where I really belong." The very core of my heart tells me that there is something disturbingly wrong about this philosophy. Especially when you and I both know that this preacher will die of old age just like the rest of us will, as will our children, their children, and their children. A physical location somewhere in outer space called "heaven" is not our home. Earth is our home. Right here, right now. (End of excerpt from *Field of Grasshoppers*)

"Sowing seeds of doubt"?

Someone recently asked me, "Ken, why are you cutting down other people's beliefs like this?" They added, "You are sowing seeds of doubt." But is doubt a bad thing? Isn't doubt an important part of the exploration and discovery process? Do we really "follow Jesus"? Or do we follow the church's translations of Jesus? Are we really truth seekers, or more accurately, religion keepers?

What does "embracing Jesus" mean to you? Does it mean embracing the truths and profound teachings that are attributed to him, or does it mean embracing an actual magical-propertied cosmic Entity who did magical-propertied acts with magical-propertied blood that has magical-propertied power over Adam's ancient magical-propertied, voodoo-like curse to accomplish magical-propertied results in your life? Believe it or not, the latter is what millions of people were taught to believe. And yes, they believe in their hearts that they "know" the (actual) person Jesus on the same social level as one can know a co-worker.

Is it "the truth" (translation: naked reality) that sets us free, or is it a magical-propertied Jesus PERSON who sets us free - in a magical-propertied, mythological-like fashion? Did Jesus ever say that he would set us free? I don't think he ever did. I think he said the *TRUTH* will. I also think that most objective-minded people could find several first-century private conversations between Jesus and his friends that have been made into totally-misinterpreted, global State-of-the-Union type speeches that never took place.

I know these are questions that so many people want to stay completely away from. But all I'm really asking for here is some concentrated brutal, inward honesty...

A very dear neighbor describes her experience like this...

"Yes, it is all about finally trusting our own hearts, our own logic, intuition, and deductive reasoning 'as if' they were luxuries instead of enemies... It was impossible for me to understand how these characteristics were celebrated in day to day life, yet the same characteristics were the 'work of the devil' when used to ponder religious stories/ideas. I still remember vividly sitting in our car at the airport. I had just received a popular Christian book from my grandma, and my mom was asking me about it. I told her I had stopped reading it (due to discomfort) because it was actually making me question more. My belief system was being shaken by a book that was supposed to strengthen it. When I gave her examples and began to question aspects about the Bible or 'our' religious history, it was made clear that those were not thoughts coming from God. I asked 'but didn't He make me who I am? Didn't He give me this brain, to think deeply about, evaluate, and question any information that I come in contact with?' No - that was now somehow the devil sneaking in.

It just never made sense how I should use such logical skills to solve every day problems, but should not use those skills when thinking about religion. It's like here: take this little pill, become a zombie, and just believe everything we say. If you don't do this willingly like a good Christian then we are going to have to throw fear and guilt based messages in your direction to coerce you into such.

It is just all so contradictory. Whether it be messages and stories in the Bible, or the way we are to carry ourselves in the modern world. Everything contradicts. And I have a hard time getting on board with that."

Honesty brings clarity

The songs and philosophies I have displayed in this chapter are my absolute sincere attempts to unveil an underlying problem in a belief system I finally left, with the hope of bringing some honest clarity as to why I left.

My goal with this book is hopefully to inspire people to start thinking their *own* thoughts and coming to their *own* conclusions, rather than just nostalgically adopting the writings of ancient men, or trustingly adopting whatever translations they were given of those writings. I want all my fellow humans to wake up one morning and truly realize that we (here in the twenty-first century) are every bit as "inspired" as a bunch of old Jewish religious men from thousands of years ago. And why wouldn't we be? I mean… let's really think this through rationally… We are being asked to "just believe" there was some ancient, isolated Mediterranean tribe – where literally dozens of Jewish men were in direct communication with the Creator of 500 billion galaxies… to the extent of being used (by this God) to write the many (supposedly-God-dictated) books of the Bible. But, millions of other good men from all the other continents and cultures of our planet? Um… not so much. Really?

It is my most sincere contention that our inherited, mental reliance upon a Power somewhere outside of ourselves, even in light of all the good religion has done, is in the long run an actual inhibitor of the growth and societal evolution everyone really longs for. Everyone wants world peace and to see all the peoples of the earth eventually living in harmony and unity with one another. Who among us really thinks that some sort of us-versus-them conversion contest between the world's two biggest religions will ever lead us to such peace? Let's be honest… until religion is gone, such a "kingdom" here can never, and will never happen.

There is only one way we can ever be "one,"
and that is when we all finally realize
that we already ARE.
We all share the same birth, life, and death,
and whatever lies beyond that.

I know there are some who will actually experience inner pain from reading things like this, due to their emotional or ... nostalgic connection to their religion. And again, what do all these song lyrics have in common? When God doesn't do what we've been told He does, and doesn't act like the God we've been told He is – we are being asked to just ignore those uncomfortable facts of life, and believe anyway. If things work out for us then there's our "proof." If things don't work out, then "there must be some deeper reason why God is doing something else for us." But coming to public, honest grips with the actual evidence is not an option. Why? If we allow observable reality to dictate reality, our inherited religious beliefs will suffer a deconstruction that is much too uncomfortable to bear. The idea of losing a Daddy in the sky is just too high of a price to pay, so observable reality is discredited or explained away in whatever manner we can dream up.

I was finally willing to ask the irreverent questions and concede to the outlandish-to-some conclusions... No matter how euphoric-sounding the harmony or heartfelt lyrics of these songs might seem, as they did to me for decades, as they chant in somber unison about things like "glory" or "mercy" or "redeemed," or the strange romancing of an obviously-unproductive, ultra-dependent relationship with a God, wherein every week is a struggle; this could all be factually wrong, and simply a mythology-like narrative that has been accepted and adopted as literal for millions of people.

In a song called, "Your Love Is wild," the singer chants these words of adoration to God...

"Your love, a mighty river
Your grace, a raging sea
Your mercy knows no measure
As it crashes over me..."

And yet... there's Auschwitz, the children's cancer ward, special-needs kids, and the tsunami of 2004 and 2011. And so... as God's mercy is crashing over this religious musician, a million cubic tons of seawater are crashing over the shores of Japan, killing 15,891 innocent people. When humans BEG God for mercy but no mercy comes, all those romantic-sounding lyrics become just that – romantic-sounding lyrics. Explaining these stark, uncomfortable facts away in lofty, literary style has actually become somewhat of an art form in church circles among theologians and scholars. And what am I doing here? I'm just a guy, standing here on the ground, asking for people's honesty. That's all. And for some folks, such an exercise is actually painful.

More depressing Christian song lyrics

When confusion is my companion
And despair holds me for ransom
I will feel no fear
I know that You are near

When I'm caught deep in the valley
With chaos for my company
I'll find my comfort here
'Cause I know that You are near
You carry my weakness, my sickness, my brokenness all on Your shoulders
Your shoulders
My help comes from You
You are my rest, my rescue
I don't have to see to believe that
You're lifting me up on Your shoulders

And yet… if a loving father actually did lift us up on his shoulders, would we say things like, "I don't have to see or feel that I'm up here to believe I am."? We would know if we were being carried on the shoulders of a loving father, would we not? Again, songs like this, and life philosophies like this ring much louder as comfort-based romance than actual, honest-to-ourselves reality. We believe the narratives we were told to believe, and again… mainly for one reason - because they are comforting. Isn't that the actual truth we don't want to hear or accept?

Yes, every one of us

We all go through tough times in life, ALL of us, both theist and atheist alike. And we all have the natural ability to work through (emotionally, mentally, and philosophically) any issues or challenges life presents. Then there's this...

1. A young agnostic or atheist mother loses her child at age 3, and 6 months later her dad dies, and it is so hard for her that she loses her job over it.

2. A young Christian mother loses her child at age 3, and 6 months later her dad dies, and it is so hard for her that she loses her job over it.

Both of these people have moments of indescribable despair, and both of them also experience several episodes of unexplainable strength and even inner peace when they feel like the grief is just too much to handle. Yes, both of them. The Christian woman attributes this to an invisible friend who is a Daddy-like "God" carrying her on His shoulders, as it were. The agnostic or atheist woman is simply blown away by her ability to overcome very difficult times, and is just as grateful as the Christian woman for these amazing moments of mysterious, inner strength. The Christian woman is grateful *to*, but the atheist or agnostic woman is grateful *for*. Both women have someone show up at the door just at the right time to encourage them - with just the right words. The Christian woman attributes this to "answered prayer," and the other woman says out loud, "Wow! We all really ARE somehow connected to each other. This is not only honesty, this is observable reality. Every family on earth (atheists and theists alike) have experienced this in full. Oh yes, they have.

In reality, there is no invisible friend who "carries us on His shoulders" (not literally or figuratively or spiritually or metaphorically), but simply positive thinking and believing things will somehow work out, and attracting/manifesting the results of that energy, regardless if that narrative has elusive cosmic heroes in it or not. And no amount of euphoric-sounding music or a thousand people chanting "His grace is sufficient for me" is going to make an actual anthropomorphic

Being a reality. We get through difficult things in life because that is how amazing WE are, not how amazing some completely-hidden-from-us Entity outside of ourselves is. And we have all been warned of the "dangers" of having such "pride" in our own abilities.

> *"Chanting is no more holy than the murmur of a stream,*
> *counting prayer beads no more sacred than simply breathing.*
> *If you wish to attain oneness with the Tao,*
> *don't get caught up in spiritual superficialities."*
>
> *- Lao Tzu*

Is there really an actual Boss-Mechanism/Hierarchy ... "King" who "shakes the whole earth with holy thunder and leaves us breathless in awe and wonder"? No. This is romance and poetry at its very religious best. And once again, it is all about one main thing – comfort from a Santa-like Being that is more inconsistent in character than any earthly dad is. We don't like to admit it to ourselves, but "God" is an ancient EXPLANATION for why things sometimes work out wonderfully for us, rather than realizing that normal, natural life has both ups and downs – mixed in with law-of-attraction dynamics that we have yet to fully explore and comprehend.

And so this God remains (in so many minds) as a "loving Father," and as a friend who is "closer than a brother," even though that character sketch cannot consistently show itself to be true to that model in any reasonable level of honesty. Is this not a "belief" that is based on hope in a "reality" that in all actuality is a comforting *alternative* to reality?

> *What needs to increase is NOT more doctrine-based "revelation"*
> *about "what certain ancient scriptures really mean,"*
> *but our brutal, naked honesty about what vivid,*
> *observable reality already so clearly shows us in such simple,*
> *measurable, documentable, comprehendible fashion.*

The Prime Directive

If the God of the Bible is real, then "He" is obviously hiding from us, but why? Have you ever wondered about that? In the television series, Star Trek, Star Fleet Command has a rule called The Prime Directive... It states that no one aboard the Star Ship Enterprise can ever be visibly identified by any of the intelligent life forms on any planet in any galaxy. Are we to believe that a God has decided to live by such a rule?

Confessions of a free man

Apparently we are just supposed to accept that a God hiding from us is reasonable – without even thinking that through. But why is God hiding? Why would a God hide from his creation? How could that make sense? Why would it be better that way? Is there really a God who hides from us in a secret, also-hidden spiritual kingdom? Or is everything anyone (educated or not) ever needed to know sitting right out in front of us like a huge oak tree in the middle of a hundred-acre field? Imagine that. That would be ... too easy?

    I have been fighting the brutal honesty of my heart (with my indoctrinated mind) all of my adult life. Some finally surrender to the truths of their own heart, which then so gently and so nakedly and so easily presents them with a life philosophy that harmonizes perfectly with observable reality and nature. We call these kinds of people "lost." But, ironically, life philosophies that require libraries full of thick books explaining why their beliefs don't harmonize with observable reality and nature are called "found." And millions prefer this more complicated model, mainly because it comes with promises of comfort and warm, Mommy-like hugs, with the extra bonus of being able to judge people and their status with a God, not to mention a safe and secure afterlife.

    Surrendering to reality has always seemed like the logical thing to do, hasn't it? Have you ever wondered why that is? Maybe, just maybe, there really is nothing hidden that we must dig and search and study for. Maybe that whole "studying to show ourselves approved" thing is not the "easy yoke" at all... but rather the hard one, the frustrating one, the confusing, conflicting, contradictory, continually perplexing, and perpetually striving one... in the hopes of someday finally being able to convince ourselves of some hopefully-valid doctrine-based permission to see ourselves as significant... and then, on top of that, for some reason that we don't really deserve.

Maybe that is why there are thousands of different denominations built upon the same exact collection of ancient writings. Maybe it is nature that is oh so naked and clear and readable by every human regardless of culture or station in life. Maybe it is nature that is never-changing, always consistent, same-yesterday-today-and-forever, and quite literally treating every life form exactly the same... with no prejudice toward anyone for any reason.

Maybe we are *already* significant, and always were. And maybe reality is enough, and all we really need. And maybe, just maybe, reality is the truth... the truth that sets us free. And maybe we don't need comforting alternatives for it. Maybe acceptance and appreciation for what clearly is - is enough. Maybe our own humanitarian love and the love we receive from other humans is enough love. Is that even possible? Or are there really religion-based, judicial rules for this particular planet from some particular God? Maybe the reality is that there are no cosmic, intergalactic super-heroes and Entities, but just ordinary people like you and I sometimes doing extraordinary things because of an extraordinary universe.

I have no problem with there being some sort of organic Life Force system that governs all life systems throughout the universe, and I don't even care if people feel the need to call that Life Force "God." But the lack of evidence is just too overwhelming for that Source to be anything like the loving, caring, protecting character sketch the church sold us. For me personally, saying that this God cares is no different than saying the sun loves and affectionately cares for the plants in our gardens, or that the ocean cares about the fish, or that the soil cares about the roots of the trees. It is a comfort-driven belief, not a fact. If it were a fact, then without a doubt this ... God cares about some folks more than others. That is what observable reality vividly shows. We cannot have it both ways.

The true motive for most Bible studies

(The never-ending search for personal significance)

After spending my entire life with my nose buried in theological studies, I simply stepped back and took a long, concentrated look at what real, everyday life out here on the ground so vividly shows. And I asked the question… "Why is a good third of my religion about making up romantic-sounding guesses and excuses for why God doesn't act like the Entity we were told He is?" And what was all the studying really about? If I can be completely honest with myself, most of my studying was about a perceived (taught) need to find my own personal significance within the onion skins of that huge book called "Bible." In truth, religion put me on this never-ending search for significance… mainly because they themselves (my mentors) also felt insignificant because of the crap they were told about themselves by *their* mentors.

> *To think of the Life Force of the Universe*
> *like religions think of their Gods,*
> *would be like assigning human characteristics*
> *to gravity, or any other natural law.*
> *- Jim High*

My friend, Kevin Sturges recently said, "After many years of painful study, introspection, and self-honesty, that's the conclusion I came to as well. I'm not some bitter, wounded Atheist. I don't hate God or even the idea of a God. I just think it's obvious that the stories and identities of any of those ancient biblical characters do not line up with reality at all. What I came up with, at least for now, is that whatever the originating force governing the rules of the universe is, It must be more like the ocean… magnificent, beautiful, life giving, but terribly and remorselessly cold and impersonal if you get too close or stand in its awe inspiring way. It goes where it wills. It does what it sees fit, for its own, as yet for impervious reasons."

Reloaded Mercies

The sun obviously provides energy for the plants, just as other suns do for hundreds of billions of other planets. But all those stars/suns don't "love" the planets that orbit them. There is a Bible verse that says God "feeds the birds." But would a God literally feed the birds and not the starving children? Is this verse not more appropriately saying that nature provides for even the birds? The ancient Jews, like many cultures before them, thought nature was an actual "Person," or in some religions, "persons." But does that make it so? One of my religious friends shared a picture of a sunrise the other day with the Bible verse that states, "God's mercies are new every morning." Now does that mean there is some sort of … actual invisible reservoir of mercies that gets reloaded or refreshed every time our regional area gets hit by the rays of the morning sun? Or is this more about the fact that we as humans can get a new outlook on things with every new day – a quite natural occurrence that any good night's sleep can offer?

Is there a reason for our … need of some mystical/spiritual explanation for why we overcome a rough day at work or a challenging life circumstance? If there is, then it is undoubtedly a taught need, not a natural need. Why? Because nature already answers these questions quite easily. Why would we need to turn normal, everyday natural life into something so weird and spooky? The answer? Once again… comfort.

Funny thing about reason (and reasons)

It was reason that finally ridded me of some taught "need" to have a hundred "reasons" for a hundred different things in life. When I finally recognized that the need to have so many reasons was actually motivated by an underlying (completely undetected) fear and insecurity of not having all the correct reasons and translations and interpretations and explanations and "answers" - it was also easy to finally let go of such a huge, heavy bag of theological dot connecting. What's more is that none of it was ever necessary in the first place. Even more fantastic than that is the fact that so many of those so-called reasons were simply hopeful alternatives to the harsher realities of nature. Have I mentioned that yet? I know I have.

And so, rather than facing reality head on, and with courage, understanding, and acceptance, I sought out comforting "reasons" that assisted my denial-of-reality issues. And religion was more than willing to help. Shocking as this may be to some, nature offers all the reasons you will ever need. And that's actually the truth. It is the truth we don't want to be true, but the freedom thereof cannot be tasted without it. There is no secret "plan" for your life, unless you have a rich uncle or something. The only planner is YOU. Yes, it is all you, and it is all on you – your responsibility to do whatever you wish with your life. Some people find such freedom scary and insecure. Perhaps the healthier road is to take that responsibility seriously at 100 percent rather than pawning it off on an invisible, hiding friend. It's on you, and always was on you. And that is exciting, adventurous, full of potential, and fun.

"Something Amazing" - Ken, are you an atheist now?

(An excerpt from *What Is God, And How Does It Work*)

> A very close, extremely enlightened friend asked me this... "Ken, are you an atheist now?"
>
> My answer: "I don't think so... I'm not sure... Is that possible? Um... well, I think the term "God" could very well be a concept that ancient man used (came up with) to hopefully explain in human terms – something amazing. They experienced very real, undeniable interactions with "something"... something very predictable... so predictable that philosophies to live by could be written about it for the good of the collective. Several ancient cultures experienced this same... "something amazing," and they each gave different names and explanations for it. Some even gave several different characters for it.

If you would like I can give you a long list, because I have done some pretty extensive research on these things. Personally, I am not into titles all that much myself anymore, but some folks seem to like them very much. And I guess that's okay if one needs that sort of "certainty" to sleep by. Nevertheless, now we all call this ... something amazing - "God." And if one doesn't call this "something amazing" by its proper title, "God," then that one is "bad," and we call them a "bad atheist."

So to answer your question, I guess since I still firmly believe in "something amazing" I guess I am still luckily "free" from being a "scary atheist." But wait a minute... I have also met several atheists who also believe in "something amazing." Okay, I'm confused. Perhaps there is no such thing as an "atheist," or a "bad atheist," and it is just another title someone came up with because certain people didn't believe other people's definition or interpretation of the very real "something amazing" we all share.

It is difficult for us to admit to ourselves that almost all of our current beliefs and "understandings" of a "God" were given to us by other people (including ancient people). In addition to that - all of our experiences *with* what we now think we understand as "God" have been defined, explained, and interpreted *for* us by other people... to the extent that those inherited-from-others concepts have long since been viewed (by us) as facts, not teachings.

At this point in my personal observations, this is beyond undebatable. And yet, for some, to point out this obvious, awkward truth is ... a very unwelcomed exercise. Why are labels oh so important to us? The answer? Because they "help" us divide and separate ourselves from one another? And some actually see that as a good thing.

The Great Cosmic Joke

In an article called, "The Cosmic Joke behind Enlightenment," Chad Foreman asks the question… "Is seeing the Humor in Enlightenment the key to finding it?" He goes on to say… "The great cosmic joke is that you are what you are seeking. All the religious and spiritual seeking on this planet makes you end up back where you started. If that's not a fantastic joke worth a good belly laugh I don't know what is. We all look for happiness, peace and fulfilment in the things of the world, yet all along these things are our very nature – our very own center of being. Meditation masters and mystics throughout history have seen the joke of it as Zen Master Thich Nhat Hanh explains: 'I laugh when I think how I once sought paradise as a realm outside of the world of birth. It is right in the world of birth and death that the miraculous truth is revealed. But this is not the laughter of someone who suddenly acquires a great fortune; neither is it the laughter of one who has won a victory. It is, rather, the laughter of one who; after having painfully searched for something for a long time, finds it one morning in the pocket of his coat.'"

Five
THE UNIMAGINABLE

What I am asking my readers to do here is to imagine the absolute unimaginable – that there actually is a chance that most of what religion has taught us about a God could very possibly be completely inaccurate to reality. And I am asking my readers, if at all humanly possible; to consider the possibility that humankind was not born into some Harry-Potter-like "spiritual" darkness wherein we inherited a need for some sort of legal-based acquittal for the "crime" of being born as some sort of … sinful, unclean, undeserving, ugly, forever-indebted, law-breaking, not-quite-good-enough human. The deer, the aardvark, the eagle, and the butterfly do not suffer from these delusions. Only we humans have been sold such dark, disempowering, science-fiction-like insanity about our species… all based on some ancient religious writings of a rather small regional Mediterranean culture – which is also based heavily on *their* own (ancient-to-even-them) tribal-like Judaic laws and concepts of how the operational dynamics of the universe actually work. Whew!

Their "findings"? It's a "Guy." And this conclusion was not new, for this whole Zeus-like, Guy-in-the-sky, out-there-somewhere, separate-from-ourselves, invisible-Entity-concept had even more ancient roots from Greece, Egypt, the Great North, and the Far East (please refer to *What Is God, And How Does It*

Work). This is a very uncomfortable subject for some to exert even a little objectivity on and do their own, unsupervised due-diligence research. And that is precisely why so many choose not to. The Jews were actually quite late in the game of selling their Santa-like God-concepts as a fact. And yet the naive beliefs of many are that this ancient Jewish tribe was the first, and that Adam and Eve were (literally) the beginning of all human history. Well, we now know that the first signs of humans date back to at least 200,000 years ago. It is not information that we lack, but the desire to thoroughly investigate it all. The most recent discoveries of manmade tools are now pushing those numbers to over a million years ago. Few people know that the biblical version of the creation story itself was a borrowed-and-revised story of an even more ancient culture of the Babylonian Enuma Elish. I didn't know that. Did you know that? Is this "just another" one of those 100 things that don't really matter?

The Origin Trap

"My Daddy can beat up your Daddy!" said the little girl who felt she might be losing the argument with the neighborhood kid about whether or not tadpoles turn into frogs. Now think about that for a moment... What does anyone's dad have to do with frogs and pollywogs? I'll tell you what... emotion. When people are emotionally invested in being right no matter what, conversations can very often end up in places that have nothing to do with the original subject.

I can't tell you how many times when having a conversation about God's character compared to observable reality when someone straightaway shifts the subject to a creation/evolution debate. This really puzzled me for the longest time, because it was beginning to become almost predictable. Eventually I understood what was happening. By revealing to someone that the God they were sold is not as accurate to reality as they had been convinced, they experience a most uncomfortable fear of losing something very dear to them... an ideology that guarantees comfort, and on many levels. I think if we can be brutally honest with ourselves we will discover that our desire to maintain a hierarchy Boss mechanism "God" is mostly about two main things... comfort and judgment.

Our license for judging our neighbor disappears without a God, and our escape from (and denial of) nature also demands a God Who makes a way around the dying process, offers us spiritual "reasons" for the everyday challenges of life, and gives us a supernatural maternal Entity that we can believe is working things out on our behalf behind the scenes.

One afternoon when asking someone to consider the uncomfortable reality of their God not saving a drowning child, or a lost hunter, or not healing a crippled person, they quickly responded with, "So Ken, are you one of those who believe the universe just accidentally came about because of some big bang? If so, we have no purpose, no meaning, no reason for living, and no consequences for our actions. With that belief we are then no better than a mere animal that lives and dies and then ceases to exist."

Did you see that?

1. The conversation completely flipped from an honest discussion about God's biblical character sketch to a discourse about whether or not there is a God who makes galaxies, birds, alligators, and mosquitos.
2. If evolution is true then that somehow equals no purpose or meaning for anything.
3. If evolution is true then there's no reason for living and no consequence for our actions.
4. Animals are "mere" animals, and cannot live forever somewhere in outer space like us.

Another person named Larry said this, "So Ken, what are you saying? Are you saying that we are just here for no particular reason, like ants on a hill running to and fro? That's a very sad view, Ken, and wholly unnecessary. Such an atheistic view leaves the universe a cold, lonely place that presents the ever-present possibility that the 'Big Bang' could eventually evolve into the 'Big Crunch,' as all that exists could then fold together on itself and just vanish. Ken, the 'Life Force System,' as you call it is GOD, whether you seek to deny His existence or not."

I have three questions for Larry...

1. What does acknowledging a "Him" God accomplish? The honest answer is the (believed) favor of this God because of one's acknowledgment, wherein people have been convinced that by paying this God compliments we have the ability to make this God happy/pleased with our thoughts and actions. The unspoken, even denied belief, is that if we make God happy, then He will make us happy. If we can be honest, this is the essence of that belief system in a nutshell. We can call it all sorts of romantic things like "walking in covenant," etc, but the guts of the whole thing is very much like a wife striving to please her demanding husband.
2. If one does not continuously acknowledge or thank a God for the air they breathe, does ice cream taste differently, does the kiss from a lover lack intensity, can they not also live a life full of purpose and beauty and meaning, and will they still cry tears of joy at the birth of their first child?
3. Why does there need to be mythology-like "reasons" for being born on this planet with millions of other life forms? As I have stated before, although religious folks won't say this out loud... they believe as they were told to believe - that one of the biggest 'reasons' we are here is to get safely to somewhere else. Imagine that. Again, if we can make a God happy with our correct beliefs, He will give us eternal life. But, if we don't, He simply cannot allow it. Again, this book you are reading is a book about brutal honesty of the heart.

When conversations get turned on their heads like this there is always someone who will start trying to prove the existence of a God. Their argument is often well-versed and even intelligent, as they speak of things like "design" requiring a "Designer," natural law requiring a "Law Giver," and other assertions about morality, free choice, and the origins of good and evil, etc. And I almost forgot the one about how "God must be true to His Word..."

But what is really going on here? What are they really trying to protect and preserve? I hate to be so redundant, but the answer to that question, again, is...

comfort, and to some, judgment is equally as important. They cannot imagine all of a sudden losing their license to judge others.

When people are suddenly faced with the possibility of losing some of their religion-based comfort (or judgment) a sort of rapid-fire, emotion-based rebuttal mode kicks in, wherein they reach for anything they can to hold on to. Unfortunately, neither the evolution camp or the creation folks have even the slightest clue of exactly how our universe came about. The evolutionists say, "We think something went BANG," and the creationists say, "No. It was a GUY!" Excuse me, but no one on either side of this debate is taking that cake home any time soon.

Bottom line? It does not matter how we came about. It doesn't matter at all. We cannot make our Source happy or pleased with us, nor cause (in any way whatsoever) that Source to individually reward us in any way because of our actions or beliefs or thoughts... Why? Because IT (or "God") is not a Santa-Claus-like "Person," or ... anthropomorphic-like personality. This has never been the case, and I think that many of us have somehow always known this in our hearts.

Where we actually live

What we all do know is that there are anywhere from 300 billion to 500 billion other galaxies (the latest numbers from NASA are tripling that), all of which contain 100 billion or more solar systems much like our own. NASA announced on May 10, 2016 that the Kepler Space telescope has located 1,284 exoplanets orbiting hundreds of our closest stars/solar systems. At least 43 of those planets have been found to be within what is called the "Goldilocks," or "Habitable Zone," which is in a similar relation to their sun as our planet is to our sun – where biological life is thought to be very possible. On November 4, 2013, astronomers reported, based on the amount of Kepler's data so far, that there could very well be as many as 40 billion Earth-like planets just within our own galaxy, orbiting their suns in the habitable zone. Something else we now know is that the orbital mechanics in hundreds of billions of other galaxies operate on the same exact natural laws we observe here in our tiny corner of our own galaxy. We can now estimate interstellar events hundreds of light years from here with a great degree of predictability. This subject is discussed in an expansive fashion in my second book, *What Is God, And How Does It Work.*

When I personally came to grips with just the size and scope alone of our known universe much of my inherited theology began to move into a very precarious position – wherein I was now forced to add logic, reasoning, and a healthy dose of rational honesty to many of the mythology-like narratives I had been taught. Back when stars were "pretty sparkly things," and galaxies were "big spiral-like objects in outer space" my theology could still sort of ... make sense to me. Because back then I lived on a planet that was not only at the center of our galaxy, but the very beginning of the universe. All the stars, the moon, and the sun, according to the Bible anyway, were "made" by an Invisible Being specifically to give light to the earth (even though 99.9 percent of all stars in the universe cannot be seen or shed any light on our planet or our galaxy). This ... "God-Guy" supposedly had a "boy," and well... you know the rest of the story.

However, what is more than baffling to me is why an omnipotent Creator would create an entire galaxy for "His chosen children" to inhabit only 0.000000000000000000015% of its area, for only 0.00004% of its history.

We now actually know that not only is our planet nowhere near the center of our galaxy, but that our galaxy is nowhere near the center of the known universe. Which makes one wonder if our universe is anywhere near the center of a billion other universes. Long story short, like the wizard behind the curtain in the movie *The Wizard of Oz*, there is... p r o b a b l y not a Supreme King, Ruler, Boss-mechanism "Guy" who had a boy, or wanted a dead animal as a sacrifice from some certain tribe in the Middle East for breaking "His" religious laws. Is that too ... harsh of a conclusion? I am willing to bet my next paycheck that whatever energy source brought about 500 billion galaxies does not have a favorite religion in one of those galaxies, or in one of that particular galaxy's 100 billion solar systems – where there happens to be one particular atmosphere-protected exoplanet that its inhabitants call "Earth." We really don't like thinking about things like this, do we? After all, we can't have Jesus (God's only boy) dying in 500 billion different galaxies on a kazillion other habitable-zone exoplanets, can we? To combat such an uncomfortable reality we've come up with a solution...

just keep seeing the universe as nothing more than "really big" rather than actually having seriously-honest, rational conversations about just how big it really is, and what that probably means. Rational thinking on such matters is not encouraged in some circles.

Alone in the universe? I think not

The idea that we are alone in the universe is arrogant at the very least. Some theologian's and "Christian scientists" have recently 'decided' that the habitable conditions of earth can be the only template in which life can survive on any other planet in the entire universe. I wish I was making this up. In light of the fact that we have life forms here that thrive in deep-sea hydrothermal vents spewing out water at 400C onto the ocean floor, these "scholars" are obviously trying to establish something theological, not scientific. Our garden variety frog can literally freeze solid as a block of ice and then somehow come back to life in the spring. The Red Flat Bark North American beetle can survive - 148 degrees F (- 100 degrees C). If we assume that intelligent life on other planets must have an atmosphere exactly like ours to sustain life, we are really limiting what nature can do. Our own planet should be enough of a testament of that. I do not have proof, but I am very optimistic that there are billions of planets with oceans literally teaming with biological life, and land creatures – some of which have built things that would make our latest technology look like our first attempts at blacksmithing. What's more is that there is probably intelligent life out there living in environments that we couldn't even breathe in.

Think about this, if you can... We need a good supply of oxygen in order to venture out into the unknown. Imagine a species somewhere much more advanced than us who live under the waves of a yellow ocean – who need a good supply of toxic-to-us liquid filling their cabin space in order to travel out away from their home planet. Since we cannot imagine such things we decide that they are impossibilities. But what the bleep do we know?

Six

GOD'S NOT DEAD IF "HE" NEVER EXISTED

A good Christian friend of mine, who has been in a continual conversation about these things for about five years, asked me, "Ken, are you saying that no one fully knows God who exists independent of us? Or are you saying that finite human beings actually created an infinite God? Do you believe in God? What kind of God is one that we make up in our own heads? That reduces God to a fairy tale. My answer, of course, was, "How can one reduce something that in reality may not actually exist in the first place?" The big word here, once again, is blindly-accepted PREMISE.

If you'll notice in his questions – the matter-of-fact style in which the questions are asked… It is very difficult for him to grasp what is even being said when someone from outside of his faith is questioning the very existence of a God. So when I suggested the possibility of ancient humans "creating" a God in their own image, my friend immediately tries to figure out how I would believe that mere humans could possibly create an (actual) infinite God. You see, for my friend, in his mind, the existence of a God is an established "fact." And in the minds of many other believers this God is also very much like themselves… gets angry, happy, sad, pleased, etc. And why wouldn't they think that? Because that is the anthropomorphic character sketch their Bibles present.

But what I meant was that ancient humans CONCEPTUALIZED a quite Zeus-like Entity that was thought to be dwelling up in the sky somewhere. We see several pieces of evidence of this ancient belief peppered throughout the Bible… In the Psalms we hear David talking about "his help" coming from *up* in the hills. At one place a man and his chariot flew *up* into the sky (the heavens) to be with God. Jesus was said to have floated *up* into the sky (to heaven)… And where does the fierce, powerful sound of thunder come from? From the sky 'up above.' Where does the frightening bolts of lightning come from that splits the mighty oak in half? The skies 'up above' us. From where does the rain that waters our crops come from? From the same place our warmth from the sun comes from… 'up above.' It should be no surprise that ancient men from places like Greece, Rome, Egypt and India conceptualized very human-characteristic-like, anthropomorphic Beings and Entities, like patriarchal "Fathers" who provided everything needed (as patriarchal fathers actually did in those days). Again, this is a book about honesty. Are lightning strikes really precision-planned by a God, or are they natural products of the weather – governed by very impersonal laws of nature? Are the thunder claps the emotions or the premeditated display of a God's displeasure, or are they merely the effects of warm air mixing with cooler air?

In the minds of some, any serious questioning of whether there actually is a God is viewed almost as a crime of some sort. The thought process of many believing theists is, "How stupid can atheists be not to believe in a God?" This same group of theists, however, never stop for even a minute to do some honest research on the history of where their own beliefs came from. Did they (actually) see a God, or did they (actually) hear a God? In the church I grew up in there was a spiritual reason authoritatively given for almost everything imaginable. Bad day at work? The devil is trying to steal my joy. Marital challenges? The evil one doesn't like happy marriages. Good day at work? God is blessing me, and I am "truly blessed." When things worked out wonderfully – God was answering my prayers. When my prayers were not being answered – God perhaps knew that my request was not the best thing for me at that time. I was told that this God would never give me more than I could handle. When my nephew lost his wife to cancer he said, "I guess God knew I could handle losing my wife, but the guy in the room across the hall (also praying for his wife) obviously couldn't handle losing his wife, because she recovered." His statement, of course, was made in contempt of the idea that there is a God who allows some to die and others to live. Does religion offer "answers" for this? No. Again, they offer guesses. And those guesses are more about preserving and maintaining inherited beliefs than they are about getting to the bottom of honesty or truth about reality. Can we be totally honest about this?

A girl named Linda recently said to me, "Ken, I'd like to hear what your God *is* rather than what your God is *not*." My answer, although perhaps a bit shocking to some, is this… "I do not have a 'God,' and I don't believe anyone else does either. I think what we *do* have is a thousand different *explanations* called 'God,' most people being quite sure of themselves that they have the correct version. In my lifetime, between the 60's and the 90's a very slim minority believed that 'God' could justifiably be nature itself. But just within the last decade alone those numbers have changed drastically. More and more people are abandoning so many of their inherited Guy-in-the-sky models of 'God,' and are beginning to be very open-minded about other viable options. Scary? Not really.

If we actually think we can make a God either happy or sad with our thoughts and beliefs, we have not been taught love, but fear. If we think we have to be … careful of what we secretly believe or what we say out loud about a God, then we are more interested in the fear of our own eternal safety than we are about truth. Perhaps it is the raw, brutal honesty of our own hearts about reality that we fear the most, mainly because it so often sharply conflicts with the fear we have been taught is "love."

"It's alright, boy, we told you what to dream!"

Do we really need chapter and verse of ancient men's thoughts and concepts in order to live life to the fullest? Is that the truth, or is that something we were taught based on the fears and insecurities of other people?

Basically all of my interactions and life experiences with the operational dynamics of the universe were authoritatively defined *for* me as being an actual social "relationship" with a very anthropomorphic, Santa-like GUY-in-the-sky, if you will. And as a quite human-characteristic "Guy" He could be made happy/pleased by my thoughts and actions or sad/displeased by my thoughts and actions. I certainly didn't want to "let Him down," so I tried my best to do only the things that could make Him happy and pleased with me. And, naturally, once a young person is injected with such an unquestionable *premise*, every life experience is translated *through* that construct... to the extent that it actually becomes a "fact" in the mind. This ... "certainty," because of having a great deal to do with comfort, becomes a "strong tower" that cannot even be challenged by reality itself. The believer's rationale? "Observable reality be damned! My God is an awesome God. He reigns from heaven *above*! How do I know? I just do!"

But what is true because it is actually true, and what is true because we *want* it to be true? Likewise, do we know the difference between taught needs and natural needs? Is it even possible that we have been convinced some taught needs are natural needs? If so, such taught needs could actually be delaying our personal growth. Do we all have to deal with this uncomfortably-naked reality? Well... not if we don't want to. Is the answer telling ourselves lies about nature, or inventing comforting alternatives to it, or is it more about accepting things for what they clearly show themselves to be? Each of these scenarios tend to satisfy different people, but sweet, little lies, regardless of how sweet, tend to run out of sweetness in time. And once found out, they are not only walked away from, but often in frustration and mistrust towards those who (unknowingly) taught the lies.

Honesty about good and evil

> *"Is God willing to prevent evil, but not able?*
> *Then He is not omnipotent.*
>
> *Is He able, but not willing?*
> *Then He is malevolent.*

> *Is He both able and willing?*
> *Then whence cometh evil?*
>
> *Is He neither able or willing?*
> *Then why call Him God?"*
> *- Epicurus (341 to 270 BC, Athens Greece)*

One of my valued South African friends shared this commentary... "My views of good and evil and morality differ from most of the religious points of view. Let's look at it this way:

1. God exists

2. God is omnipotent, omniscient, and perfectly good as so many believe.

3. A perfectly good being would want to prevent all evils.

4. An omniscient being knows every way in which evils can come into existence.

5. An omnipotent being who knows every way in which an evil can come into existence has the power to prevent that evil from coming into existence.

6. A being who knows every way in which an evil can come into existence, who is able to prevent that evil from coming into existence, and who wants to do so, would prevent the existence of that evil.

7. If there exists an omnipotent, omniscient, and perfectly good being, then no evil exists.

8. Evil exists."

She continues...

"One of my biggest fears when I walked away from my religion and my taught concept of God was who would I become without that God. I have found that answer in and for myself. I don't need a God or a religion to have morals, a caring heart, or a purposeful life.

Some people say that if evil exists it is our problem not God's? Am I right to assume they then only attribute all that is good and right to their God? Wouldn't that then mean if we are His creation and are in some ways flawed that He could have foreseen it and prevent it if He knew the amount of suffering we would cause others and the natural world around us? I mean He is believed to be this almighty Being that created the universe and everything in it. But what about the innocent children who are being born into this world deformed just to suffer? And if you say the Christian God is only good then I also have to ask if you know your Bible? Do you also pick and choose the verses that resonate with you and ignore the rest? Personally I can think of a million reasons not to believe, but it is not my place to say what others should believe. I'm just tired of all these copped-out answers and excuses and fairy tales that we keep feeding ourselves. Maybe life is just as simple, terrifying, magnificent, awful and beautiful as it really is. Sometimes people get sick, sometimes they heal, sometimes they don't. Sometimes you can help someone and sometimes you can't. Sometimes you get killed by someone else, sometimes you don't. Just like the lion and the Impala. Nothing more, nothing less! What if this is all there is? Would that be okay?"

Honesty about suffering

One of my Christian friends recently posted on social media an article about suffering, asking anyone to give their thoughts on the matter. As usual, several people suggested the usual beliefs of a God allowing certain people to suffer for reasons that are beyond our finite ability to comprehend. Most of this kind of thinking is almost always followed up by the words, "We must just trust that the

Lord knows what He is doing and knows what is best for us." Since this person was asking for feedback, I gladly offered what I believed to be the simple answer to his question... "There is suffering in the world because of nature, gravity, centrifugal force, disease, environmental ramifications, societal growth issues in our evolution as a species, and natural disasters. That is why there is suffering. It's really quite simple and has nothing to do with some God allowing certain things to happen to certain people for certain reasons."

My friend replied with, "Ken, that is your belief. But most other people are not satisfied with that answer. And for good reasons."

But why are they not satisfied with the most simple/logical answers? They are not satisfied with the simple answers because they have been primed by religion that there is some supernatural, comforting answer that supersedes the rational, sensible answers. Nature is just too damn scary and heartless, so they've gladly adopted the alternatives they were given... If a little girl dies of cancer, then God must have needed another angel in heaven. If the overweight pastor dies because of high cholesterol, it couldn't possibly have anything to do with personal eating habits. God has "called him home." ... "His work on earth was done," etc. If we didn't get the job we were praying for, then it is because God had a better job lined up for us just around the corner, etc. When our plans don't work out the way we hoped they would, then God must be working things out behind the scenes on our behalf.

These completely made-up "answers" are not answers at all. Some have said, "Maybe God doesn't see suffering the same way we do." Well, if that's so, then the examples of "loving father" and "friend closer than any brother" are not at all fitting comparisons for this God's character.

One person told me that pain and suffering is the direct cause of the "knowledge of evil" (which Adam and Eve supposedly were suddenly aware of due to their disobedience in the garden). He suggested that this is the reason for evil in the world as well as condemnation and shame. But between you and me, condemnation and shame, correct me if I'm wrong, originate from religious doctrine of "original sin." It is no secret to professional counselor's that people tend to act out the version of who they were told they are... born "sinners," etc.

1. The reason for suffering is nature and natural causes.
2. There isn't some deeper "why," nor does there have to be.
3. There doesn't have to be a King who "allows" certain people to suffer.

One of the more popular counter arguments is that suffering can be beneficial and therefore does not preclude "loving" as an attribute of God. But that is like saying it could be appropriate for a normal father who has the power to save one of his drowning children, standing back – deciding that the death of this one child could be beneficial in teaching his other children just how precious life really is. But we would all call such a man a criminal, would we not? Yes, we would. Interestingly, to this very day there are still places in some Middle Eastern cultures where a father actually is allowed such behavior over his children and wife.

A few months ago a Christian gentleman named Mark told me how God has "allowed him to suffer" excruciating physical pain for 38 years. He added… "I have no 'why's' left, only absolute trust."

This whole … "God allows" thing is a necessary invention if one is to truly maintain the belief of a caring God amidst so much observable evidence of the contrary… the "Job complex"…

Setting the sails

If there was a "purpose" for suffering, then that would have to mean that suffering was intentionally created and designed as a beneficial tool to help us grow and develop character. And yes, there actually are people who believe this. But the "purpose" of the wind is not so sailboats can use it to navigate the seas. The beauty of sailing against the wind is a discovery of how to benefit from the wind by setting the sails in a particular fashion. The wind's purpose has nothing whatsoever to do with sailing, nor was it invented by a God for sailboats. Likewise, all human suffering is about natural laws like gravity, centrifugal force, natural disasters, poor construction, human error, environmental issues, genetics, an overabundance of rainfall, etc. People die from cancer because their immune system was not able to overcome it. Even crime and war are products of nature.

Science CAN answer the questions of why people suffer... If a volcano throws a rock the size of a bus, and it lands on your car, then that is "why" you died. If a hillside gets too much rain and the hill slides down upon your home, that is "why" some of your family members died. If a lion kills a cheetah because of hunting territory issues, that is why the cheetah died.

We certainly do grow because of the many different challenges nature offers, just like any other biological life form learns of their strengths and limitations when interacting with natural laws. A deer, for instance, learns how to run down a steep hill by first falling a few times and feeling pain and suffering. Surely we wouldn't surmise that God created hills so deer could benefit from suffering.

My inherited beliefs made simple

All the years of debates and confusingly-intricate theological discourses could be wrapped up in two sentences... Something magical (but dark) happened to a couple of humans in a garden thousands of years ago somewhere in the Middle East. Then, a few thousand years later, something magical (but good) happened that made a way for people to get well from the first magical (dark) thing – that somehow magically, negatively affected every human ever to be born. And someone is pointing at my more naturalist explanation for suffering as irrational?

In a nutshell, religion seeks to come up with comforting alternatives to some of the harsher realities of nature, rather than having the raw gut stuff responsibility of simply accepting them for what they are. They even did away with the uncomfortable, natural finality of life in the dying process... "He's with Jesus now, walking among the flowers and meadows of heaven." A woman weeps uncontrollably at the graveside of her husband, blurting out the comforting words... "That's just his body...that's just his body...He is not there...He is now in the arms of Jesus..."

But is this not a picture of our fear of nature being true... to the extent of adopting religion-based comforting alternatives for nature to believe in? The believers sing, "Because He lives, I can face tomorrow..." But does that mean that if he *didn't* live they *couldn't* face tomorrow? Meanwhile, millions in the non-theist camp are facing tomorrow just fine, many with excitement for life and enthusiasm for the future. Are we ready to be honest about this?

Honesty about my Church experience

When I think back to my church days I remember this ... Most of the people standing there in a "dynamic worship service" with their eyes closed and some with their hands raised believed something ... well, "magical" was taking place... something (outside-of-themselves) "spiritual." And as we sang praises to our King we literally believed that an invisible Entity "Who" was receiving our adoration then "entered into" a sort of spiritual intercourse with us, if you will.

What was more likely taking place was a group of people, in a very-doctrinally-defined, faith-based belief in a particular religious Super-Hero narrative – with the power *of* that sincere faith, were willingly dropping all their social and mental inhibitions while completely opening themselves up (because of that sincere, corporately-shared faith) to experience a very emotional, indeed transcendental state, and also allowing the harmonizing singing, the dreamy-like keyboards, and the power of the music (and even the music style) to "usher" them into a "place" where they "let the music take them away."

I do not wish to come across as too harsh about this subject, but this section is about *my* church experience. Because of the comradery, the synergy of a few hundred people all believing the same thing (on an emotional/devotional level), and all of whom were very openly contributing to this... ritual, the results are indeed euphoric in nature. This same exact experience can be enjoyed at a good rock concert, or in a collective of any number of religious gatherings around a campfire. I know, because I was raised in the Pentecostal church my entire life, and have also attended quite a few rock concerts... many of which left me in tears of joy and a deep sense of connectedness to both the music and the people there.

The worship music, even the style of music in a charismatic worship service is chosen carefully to evoke an emotional response, as romantic lyrics guide the worshipper to pay deeply-emotional, servant-like homage to the King. And the lyrics speak of His "unspeakable beauty" and His "unfathomable love" and how He is so worthy of our songs and emotions... and "Oh to one day see Him face-to-face" in all His Radiant Glory, etc. This is all a very ... unreal to actual everyday life mindset, because within five minutes after leaving the service we are ordering french fries at the Burger King across the street from the church, not necessarily longing anymore "like the deer pants for water" to see Jesus "face-to-face," but to make sure the cook doesn't forget the onions on our burger. Do we really hunger and thirst for God like the deer pants for water? No, we don't. This is a taught desire, not a natural one. There is something..... dishonest and quite UNgenuine about this. My heart "knew" it then, but I really know it now.

All of that "we get lifted up when we praise Him" talk, in all honesty, had more to do with corporate, romantically-shared BELIEF than it did with anything "supernatural" outside of ourselves "showering us with His presence," as I once so sincerely believed. Once I started taking 100 percent responsibility and ownership of my own life, feelings, demeanor, mental health, and happiness, I realized that most of our "Higher Power" comfort, counsel, euphoric feelings and experiences (actually) come from our own thinking, feelings, emotions, beliefs, and from working things out in our minds for ourselves - as we contemplate our environment, our desires, our imagination, and our intentions.

Honesty about the 'Law of Attraction' ("prayer")

(Excerpt from Field of Grasshoppers)
What about things like "answered prayer" and "miracles"? Surely those are real events being orchestrated by a God, right? What other explanations could there be? Well, I'm glad I asked...

> The Bible, including the teachings of Jesus, were undoubtedly written and spoken in the language, context, and concepts of the times. Throughout the history of mankind, people have experienced what

they have called "God," and in their explorative enthusiasm of realizing that God has predictable character (or attributes), wrongfully concluded that this God was very much like them, and that's exactly how they wrote the entire story; thus, assigning their human attributes to their concepts of a God. But could it be that some sort of universe-wide spiritual/natural Law is actually "God"? Could it be that "God" is actually more like a 'Program' than a 'Person,' much like the operating system on your computer? Is that really such an absurd possibility? Could there be any validity to such a 'new to us,' seemingly impersonal philosophy?

Please consider this. The language we use to get what we want from our computer is a series of clicks, drags, drops, cuts, pastes, and typing of certain particular keys. If this sowing and reaping/Law of Reciprocity/very natural Law of Attraction is true, then the language we are using to get what we need and want from our Source/God/natural law is feelings, thoughts, intention, imagination, passion, desire, attitudes, emotions, expectations, and faith. "As a man thinketh, so is he." With this philosophy, every single thought is a 'prayer.' Could that actually be true? No?

Imagine for a moment that this Law/Program (we call "God") is the same molecular level 'operating system' throughout the entire universe of 500 billion different galaxies. If not, then God would not truly be the same (in all locations) yesterday, today, and forever. Is it even possible that assigning human characteristics to this unexplainable Source was the only way ancient men could somehow explain such an interactive Provision-based Law to the people of their time? It supplied them with everything they could possibly want or need. When they acted selfishly and in a fashion that was opposite of the character or 'properties' of this originating Source, they reaped the harvest of those choices; hence their concepts of continually being either 'rewarded or punished' by an actual, well, personality, or ...

Being. But what if the real story is one about natural law and an attraction-based energy-source-exchange between us and the universe? Is "God" love, or is "love/Life" God? One person suggested to me that there is only ONE "animal," and he called it "universe," all of us and everything else merely a part OF that one animal. Is that so ... crazy? If so, compared to what other version?

Knock, knock, knockin on heaven's door…

Miracles and "answered prayer" may very well not be the result of some Supreme Being making a decision on whether or not to "answer" or "heal" or "perform" a "miracle"... Truth be completely known, the very real (yet mysterious) phenomena of "divine healing" and "answered prayer" could have more to do with some sort of law-of-attraction, nature-based dynamic that is triggered by our emotions, feelings, intentions, desires, thoughts, and our faith. And bonafide "faith healers" may have more to do with certain people having clairvoyant-like "gifts" or ... abilities than explaining them as people with "a greater measure of faith." I am now convinced that prayer and even miracles will one day be scientifically proven to not have anything whatsoever to do with some God (literally) "answering" our impassioned requests.

Perhaps ancient humans, having truly experienced this (quite natural) *law* and its Father-like (reward and punishment) properties, at one point 'decided' that *it* is a 'Person,' much like the Zeus in the sky the Greeks had conceptualized, or the "heavenly gods" of Ra and Amun and Isis of the ancient Egyptians. The writers of the Bible wrote so romantically about this 'God,' as they indeed should have. And we have all benefited greatly from their work, but now we are entering a new age where even more information is being revealed... The whole "sowing and reaping" thing is much deeper and wider than we ever imagined, and I do understand how ... romantic it is to mentally process it all in a very Santa-Claus construct, because, after all — that is what we were taught from childhood. In short, there are several aspects of our own lives that are more in our own control and guidance and even manifestation than we previously thought.

If "prayer" is being "answered" by a God-Personality in much of the same way you or I would answer the telephone, then that God is certainly not a no-respecter-of-persons Entity at all, but obviously treats some people differently than others. And the answer for this that says, "Well, we don't completely understand why God answers some prayers but not others" is not a valid or intellectually-responsibly answer at all. It is merely a "we don't know" excuse not to think rationally about such things, thereby preserving our grandparent's Santa-like concepts of a very Zeus-like Boss mechanism in the sky.

Excerpt from *What Is God, And How does It Work?*

"God works in mysterious ways". That's what we say when we have no idea just exactly how "God works". All my life my heart has told me that whatever God is, it should be very simple, clear, and obvious to understand, not mysterious, hidden, contradictive, and exegetically-schizophrenic.

Religions Are Truly Amazing (Miracle Triggers)

Say whatever negative things you will about religion, but there is something beautiful about them that most non-religious people really do not understand. One doesn't have to spend much time with the sincere, honest people from five different religions to learn that they all experience the miraculous and meaningful revelations within the narratives and parameters of their beliefs.

How undeniably amazing religions really are, Christianity being one of the most remarkable. We are talking here about a system of beliefs that are not only prophetically-poetic in so many ways, but one that produces irrefutable results. Not only is Christianity a vehicle with an amazing holy book, but one that has been thickly paved with the testimonies of real-life stories about undeniable experiences. Like most religions these experiences are usually the said results of what I call "miracle triggers". Miracle triggers are certain faith-based words, rituals, intentions, or beliefs in certain events, all of which get the God-Person's attention - Who then rewards humans individually because of these faith-based protocols. I was not taught that we are "accessing" some universe-wide, eternally-fixed law-based provisions (as I now believe), but that we were "obeying" some ancient, God-dictated written procedures and protocols, and that the God-Person who "sees" or "hears" that action - then "does" an action of His own (in much of the same way an earthly father would "do" an action like buying a child a new bicycle).

These operating procedures of most religions are quite simple... 1. We, down here below, obediently follow a set of protocols, or faithfully believe in them. 2. A God, out there somewhere sees it, and then rewards us with a miracle or provision. In short, we make God happy, then He makes us happy.

One truly does not have to be dishonest about this belief system, nor do they need to feel embarrassed or apologetic about it. It is what it is, and yes, it is beautiful and even romantic in my opinion, even though I personally do not think the dynamics of it all are accurate to reality. I would be the last to deny a life with miracles that follows faith-based actions of the heart and mind, but I do now question quite earnestly the almost mythological explanations of those experiences.

Providence or Attraction?

It is not uncommon to hear Christians interweaving a "God" (that is clearly framed in their language as an Entity outside of themselves) into everyday activities… "God was so very present at the wedding!", or… "I just really felt God orchestrating the entire road trip.", or… "It was so obvious to us all how God kept our vehicle safe from the eight-car/semi-truck accident so miraculously." Unfortunately, the people in the eight cars were, um … not Christians? Was this because they were not under the same (Christian) protection? Or was it really a matter of some folks just being in the wrong place at the wrong time? If 700 homes were destroyed in a tornado, but our home was untouched, does that mean that God didn't protect the 700? Were the people in the other houses not praying? Would we even be that cruel to assume that was the reason for their suffering? Why do we not ask these questions? Because we would rather apply faith than logic, especially in situations that we can use to help bolster our belief system.

The most honest answer I have ever gotten from a religious person is… "Ken, there's just a lot of stuff we don't know… so we don't know why God does things the way He does, or why He allows certain things to happen." Such honesty, even though incomplete, is refreshing.

Ordained Moments

I vividly remember when I was active in the church culture how quite often I would just run into other Christians no matter where I traveled. So many times a "chance meeting" with a total stranger would be interrupted with the words, "You're a Christian, aren't you?" And sure enough, God "sent them" into my life at that precise moment in time for a specific reason, usually to fill a role in some sort of ministry event, etc. And it was so ... mystical. Every wonderful or unexpected thing that happened was to be seen as the direct result of some out-there-somewhere Entity moving all the pieces and guiding our every step. Every encouraging word, every positive interaction, every chance-meeting opportunity to help someone in need was seen as a song on God's guitar. In that mindset even the bad days and dry times were viewed as God (perhaps) trying to teach us something, or wanting us to learn how to trust Him in the good times as well as the bad. There was always an explanation for anything in life that didn't seem to make sense with all of the more seemingly magical days.

Now that I am no longer an active participant in that church culture, one would think that all this synergy would come to a grinding, brake-pads-need-replacing halt. Shockingly, such a magical life only increased and intensified for my wife and I. And interestingly, in our journey of a more progressive philosophy we have found ourselves experiencing those same "chance meetings" with total strangers who just "happened to be" on the same exact 'spiritual' path as we were. And since we now view our neighbors AS ourselves (no separation) we have found ourselves in more 'ministry' opportunities more frequently than we ever did as church-going Christians.

We can see so clearly now that we do attract into our lives more of not only what we believe but who we are, as well as a continual merging into others on our same frequency, as it were. To think that "God gave us a beautiful sunset this evening on the beach," and all the non-Christians on the beach are just lucky that they happen to be on the same beach as us is not correct at all. The sunset is a part of nature, and it didn't appear so gloriously because someone from a particular religion prayed for a nice sunset for their daughter's beach wedding. Our seasons of magical days are more about our choices and our thoughts than they are about an allegiance or obedience to certain religion-based beliefs, or being in some sort of ... favored-above-other-humans status with a God.

There is a reason why most religions are big on faith and "believing that you already have what you are asking for – before you have it." And there is a reason why the entire new-age movement is ecstatic about all the many law-of-attraction books now available. The ancients had also experienced this law of attraction, but interpreted it all as an invisible Zeus-like GUY in the sky. They were certain that their "prayers" for the rain their crops needed were being "answered" by a Being, and it stuck – to the extent of lasting even up until these modern times.

Owners of answers, or mysteries?

The truth is, we don't have all the answers, and are even now discovering that a great deal of the "answers" we were given are not accurate to reality at all. But we (humankind) don't like that, so we just ... sort of make things up as we go along...

Confession Time

I, Ken Dahl, sort of make up my theology and life philosophy as I go along in life... But guess what? I didn't start this model of belief-gathering techniques... It began countless centuries before the Jews or the Egyptians...

I would say... Yes, we are all guilty of this.... We make this stuff up as we go along... But I would also say this is a good thing, and how it has been done for thousands of years. Someone makes a claim, often sensible, sometimes not so much, and then everyone does their own comparative analysis of it - compared to what their current beliefs are, and compared to what real life out here on the ground shows. And with this evolving comes a lot of guessing, but also growing as every generation gets closer to reality as the centuries keep turning.

Want proof?

Go to ANY theological group page forum on social media and ask each member to give their definition of, or personal explanation for, any major doctrinal belief they strongly hold, then sit back and get ready for hundreds of differing versions. But again, this is a good thing. This is how it has always been done. Some folks just think there was only one particular ancient time zone, country, region, and tribe that were closer than anyone from any other century could ever be. But we, here in the twenty-first century are doing exactly what others did 100,000 years ago, 20,000, 8,000, 2,000, 756, 289, or 60 years ago.

Theological Reform (on steroids)

Huge-shift theological reform is here, but it is going a lot deeper than we wanted it to. Truth is funny like that, and brutal inner honesty is even "worse"...

The treasured-by-many drawing of doctrinal lines in the sand days are coming to a sorrowful close to so many right now. That idea of "life," for many, is being replaced by simple things like brotherly love and good ole humanitarian kindness. All the religion-based doctrine, regardless of how romantic, only leads to more separation and magical thinking, and the people who see this the clearest are the youth. If nothing "has to be done," then nothing has to be done. Therefore love IS all we need. Some disagree, and that's okay...

People are beginning to realize not only the futility of such things, but the delaying of our growth as a species with all the religion-based doctrine. People, and yes, especially the younger generation, are beginning to understand that there simply are "no rules" from some hierarchy Spirit that we are supposed to follow in order to make that Spirit accept us or make our way through life at a more optimum level, there are just sowing-and-reaping laws of nature to benefit from understanding how they work.

Why wouldn't we be just as "inspired" as those living thousands of years ago? For centuries scholars and theologians worked out smaller details in the faith I grew up in. But what is happening right now in the church is unprecedented...

Within my lifetime alone the Christian faith and all its fundamental doctrines will change more significantly than they have over the last 1,000 years. The fact is, such a change has already taken place just within the last two decades alone. What are your thoughts on why this is happening?

Many sects within Christianity have now decided that the views and concepts their parents held and preserved of "God" were significantly flawed, and are now offering more thoughtful views of Old Testament cultural dynamics... Again, this is actually a very good and progressive thing, but it says something about the Christian faith. Is this something we would rather not even think about, but just....um.... roll with these changes without questioning? I'm talking here about changes that seem more likely to take place over hundreds of years - taking place over only a decade or two.

Example: Penal Substitution, the several versions of atonement, differing stances on the ransom theory, the definition of "God's grace," the "kingdom," and even "sin" are right now (as we speak) being redefined and completely upgraded by a huge number of sects within Christianity. The universalists are finally, just within the last 10 years, making a strong exegetical case against the "hell" doctrine our parents believed in. The preterists have also finally achieved widespread credibility in biblical scholarly circles, bringing forth extremely valid positions of historical eschatological events - that we are now learning all took place within the end of the first century, rather than the end-of-the-world beliefs of almost 80 percent of our parent's generation. So now we learn, just within the last 10 to 15 years that Jesus is NOT coming back here physically someday... you know... on a horse... in the clouds. These are not "minor doctrinal details." These are reformations that make those of 16th-century Martin Luther look insignificant.

It's like a patchwork quilt that we just keep repairing and adding new patches to. Some folks like me have just gotten to a point where we have said.... "Holy crap... we need to step back a few miles and really look at all of this..."

There's a reason we no longer believe several things that our grandparents believed...

My friend Frank Johnson says this, "There is no element of Christianity that has not experienced the influence of doctrinal evolution. Jesus, for example, spoke from inner, direct realization when he revealed the truth about the kingdom of

God within each of us. The Apostle John, much later, presented his gospel with many statements of theology, i.e. the entire first chapter introduction, or the often-quoted John 3:16, which, of course, were not the words of Jesus. Most believers take this for granted. Then there's the concept of Trinity, three persons in one God. This is not found in scripture, but manufactured from scripture (the latter portion of the Great Commission in Matthew, for example, was actually added at a later date). It wasn't until the end of the fourth century that we see the first formal definition of the Trinity as outlined in the Nicene Creed, developed at a Church Council. The point being, we have been the recipients of 2,000 years of evolving doctrinal tradition, but rarely question any of it. Many hold to their primary orientation and church training, basically a quite academic education. The Christian faith of today looks nothing like the revelation presented by Jesus. We simply believe what we are told, without the benefit of any significant inner awareness that comes from direct realization. Hence, the academic debate continues for so many... parsing chapter and verse and passage."

Do you believe in magic?

A few weeks ago, speaking about the crucifixion, I asked a devout Christian man named Don these two questions... 1. Is Jesus still physically alive? And 2, if so, then where do you suppose he (physically) is right now?" He replied with... "Jesus ascended *up* into heaven riding on a cloud. His physical body was then changed into an eternal spiritual body exactly like his Father." He added... "If someone has any doubts about the entire Easter story, then they have really serious problems with their faith." I simply responded to him by saying, "Dear Sir, perhaps they don't have problems with *their* faith, but with *your* faith. Maybe their faith is quite intact, but simply with different parameters than yours." I asked him to please provide any Bible verses that would support his beliefs... No answer came... just the sound of evening crickets...

One of Don's friends stepped in and said, "Jesus is alive, I know, because he has changed my life in ways that are unexplainable." I politely asked him to explain to me how he knows it was actually Jesus who changed his life, and not his faith or belief in that story narrative or his own decision making on a more subconscious level... Again, the sound of crickets... When people are asked to use brutal honesty about what they believe compared to what they actually know, they often become a bit perplexed... some of whom think there is no difference between the two.

The reason many people believe that Jesus is still alive somewhere is because of 1, they have had very real life-changing experiences and shifts in behavior, but more importantly, 2. Because they have trustingly accepted and adopted their church's explanations for those very real experiences as a very alive invisible Jesus Entity "doing things in their lives." Again, once our experiences and even our feelings about them have been defined *for* us, we can actually lose our own ability to reason things out for ourselves. And the subconscious mindset is... why should we reason things out if it has already been done *for* us? But are we really that lazy and careless about our theology? Um...

Not too long ago I tried explaining this belief system to a Christian friend, who became mildly irritated by my use of the word "magic" in trying to convey (in easy-to-understand language) what I had been taught to believe. This is what I said... "I was basically taught from ancient Middle Eastern religious text that a talking snake convinced a rib-woman to eat from a magical tree, hence convincing the man from whence she came to also partake, which resulted in the spiritual DNA of all of humans that would ever be born to become magically altered into some dark, separated-from-God state, or ... curse, that from that point forward rendered all of humanity broken, incomplete, flawed, unworthy, and separated from... 'God.' This detestable condition could only be magically reversed by (the belief in) a payment to God of a human sacrifice of a very magical person, with magical blood, upon which mankind believing in this act (specifically in the resurrection part of it) would straight away give the believer the experience of a magical inner regeneration, enlightenment, awakening, re-instatement (or reconciliation) of a quite mechanically-induced, legal-based/faith-based "right-standing-with-God" and pre-talking-snake/garden-of-Eden spiritual status, not to mention secure the eligibility for a time-based 'eternal life' for when they die, which starts immediately upon this conversion date."

No preacher has ever explained the Christian faith in this fashion, but this *is* in essence what most Christians my age were told to believe. More troubling to me than this is the fact that most of my Christian peers will vehemently deny they ever believed what I just wrote.

All the things I just mentioned were not taught from pulpits as ancient religious *beliefs*, but as indisputable facts. I probably should have used the word "supernatural" rather than "magical," but the point of my colorful, and somewhat irreverent illustration was to talk honestly about a very outside-of-reality, mythological-like saga of which millions of people have been convinced to mentally process as reasonable. None of us growing up in the church ever once thought to ourselves, "Hey... Some of what we are being taught here sounds quite similar to a few of the rituals of the ancient Aztecs."

Honesty about an "inner witness"

In religious circles people are taught to believe that any part of our better nature is God or "the Holy Spirit" talking to us, or guiding us. Some call this an "inner witness of the Holy spirit." But once again this almost completely removes US from the process of being "us." I've heard it said that stress is an alarm clock that lets us know when we are attached to something that's not true for us. I like that. And I sincerely believe this is a quite natural aspect of who and what we are as humans. We call such a thing "instincts" for the animal kingdom, and "epiphanies," or ... intuition for us. But we have somehow been convinced by religious teachers that we don't possess the luxury of these very natural attributes. Many have been trained to think lesser of themselves than the absolutely astonishing life form they truly are, and religion is the biggest culprit in having accomplished such a disservice to humanity. We are the most advanced biological species on this planet, with intuitive traits like logic, deductive reasoning, split-second comparative analysis, trouble shooting, explorative-minded data processing, and decision making abilities that go far beyond the survival instincts of most animals. In fact, we are so incredible that many are actually convinced that a God is talking to them.

"God, please speak to me..."

I always wanted God to "speak to me" like so many others had claimed He was doing for them, but eventually realized that they were (basically) talking to themselves and claiming (actually believing) that the Creator of 500 billion galaxies was (actually) "talking to them." The reason, indeed the motivation for such a fantastic thing was, of course, all about the need to feel significant and valuable and important.

They were doing something quite naturally that everyone does... contemplating information and experiences and situations in life, and then gathering their thoughts on the matter and coming to personal conclusions and ideas and solutions... but then being convinced (and romanced) by preachers that what they themselves had come up with was "God speaking to them." This made them feel ... valuable. Think about it... If the Creator of the entire universe is "talking to you" that would most definitely make you feel significant and incredibly valuable, right?

Are we really ... "hearing from a God"? Or are we truthfully talking to ourselves, and thinking that our own thoughts, brainstorming, troubleshooting, and ability to come up with our own solutions and plans is "God talking to us"? The big question for so many was, "Why does God talk to others, but not me?" The answer? "He" doesn't.

Honesty about "the law"

Are you and I a first-century Jew or Gentile? No? Then who convinced people living in Tokyo or Seattle or London or Sydney that they are? Someone recently told me, and I quote... "Before Jesus all we had was the law." But things like "the law" or "the Old Covenant" or "the New Covenant" have absolutely nothing whatsoever to do with you or me. These are the belongings of ancient, first-century people in the Middle East called "Jews" and "Gentiles."

"We"? When exactly did the Capital Hill district of Seattle "have the law of Moses"? In short, they didn't... nor did a thousand years of countless generations of Native Americans living in what we know today as Montana, nor did countless generations from Japan, Russia, Australia, or China.

The word "THE" is a major part of the problem... When I hear things like "the law" or "the new covenant" or "the Old Testament," or even "the" crucifixion, the word that sticks out the most is the word "the"... The word "the" takes someone else's ancient Middle Eastern religion and makes it global... But turning the true audience-relevance from the actual first-century people into a saga about YOU is probably one of the greatest theological blunders of all human history.

Neither me nor the city of 21st-century Seattle ever "had the law" of some ancient Jew named Moses. That entire ancient, quite legal-based construct of what life is about is NOT what my life is about at all. That's not MY story, nor some sort of operations manual or ... rule book, or instruction sheet for how I should think or what I need to believe in order to experience the most optimal life here. Those ancient writings cannot in any way result in some eternal life insurance policy. This is mythological thinking at its best.

Jesus was never some magical-propertied cosmic Entity with magical-propertied blood, nor did he do some magical-propertied act to destroy some dark, magical-propertied curse. And no amount of sincere belief in any of that will yield any kind of magical-propertied regeneration of my person or life. If our lives have been greatly changed or improved because of our beliefs, it may be more about US and our belief itself... and desire and intention and resolve (regardless of a belief in a cosmic hero narrative) to better ourselves - than it is about supernatural/magical events and activities being performed by forces outside of ourselves on our behalf.

Nothing ever "had to be done" in order for you to be enough for a God, nor even for the purpose of *showing* us that we are enough. We have always been enough. If the CHURCH tells you that you're enough, just remember... they are the same source who added the words "because of"... But there is no "because of"... That's my point.

And then... this...

I love quoting actual conversations I have had with people, because it is so raw and sincere... During this same conversation with a person named, "Matthew," he wrote this to me... "Jesus died to bring an end to the law and to put out on display his grace. You see the book of Acts says that it is us who crucified Jesus, not God. We murdered love and God forgave us anyway... the crucifixion was

God allowing us to take out all our wrath and vengeance upon Him and then responding in love towards us! He says you have done got worse and I still love and forgive you."

My reply was, "I had no 'law' other than the law of nature... until my parents decided to teach me about some ancient, Middle Easterner's religious law of some guy named Moses. I'm not a first-century Jew OR Gentile, but Norwegian. I didn't murder anyone, nor did my ancestors, so I need no such 'atonement' or forgiveness. In my most sincere opinion, many people have unknowingly adopted someone else's ancient story, and made it theirs."

I do have one sincere question for Matthew... How exactly does a bunch of ancient religious Jews and a dozen soldiers from the first-century Roman Empire = "we"?

Their study is not our study

For forty long years I studied the Bible in and out, backwards and forwards, took good notes during all the "rightly-dividing-the-Word-of-truth" sermons and teachings, and fully investigated several different approaches to "using proper interpretive hermeneutics," etc. Then one day I sat on a log and asked myself, "What has all of my studying really and truthfully and honestly been about?"

Dear reader; If you have adopted someone else's ancient saga as YOUR story, that's, um...romantic and all, but audience relevance in those ancient writings is basically out the window if you've been convinced that's your story. It's not. We can learn valuable things from many different ancient sagas from their teachers, patriarchs and heroes, but deciding that they are magical-propertied procedures and protocols from a God is taking ancient history to a whole other level.

We shouldn't be afraid of nature or reality anymore. They are better, more honest friends than we may currently realize. And know this... YOU are without a doubt THE most incredible, amazing and influential person in your own life. That is not unhealthy pride, nor is it irreverent. It is truth. Reverence for our own beauty, unknown to many, is actually the door we've been looking for our entire lives, while being told, "Stay away from that door!" After all, I am "the salt of the earth and the light of the world," just as you are. Yes, you are, and always have been.

Proper Hermeneutics

"But Ken, you were obviously in a church that didn't teach you how to interpret the scriptures with proper hermeneutics."

My only response to this is – "I'm sorry, dude. I guess I just can't wrap my head around a God Who creates 500 billion galaxies giving us such a complicated, labyrinth-like puzzle to hopefully study deep enough with 'proper hermeneutics' in order to finally become that 1-out-of-40,000 denominations who got it right." One sincere fellow asked me, "But Ken, have you studied the Bible in the original Hebrew and Greek?" People like these have never even stopped to think their own rational thoughts on why their God would 1. Hide from them, and 2. Only offer them riddles and obscure truths of which require intricate, in-depth studies of original ancient Hebrew and Greek to uncover.

> *"To me there is more spirituality in a tree*
> *than in any book made from it…*
> *A spiritual approach to life is not about*
> *connecting to a different reality,*
> *it is about differently connecting to reality."*
> *- E. Le Corre*

Honesty about "freedom"

> *When I was a child I never thought of "freedom."*
> *It had not yet become a "need."*
> *It had to be taught to me…*

Later in life, in paradoxical fashion, it was actually the taught need for freedom that I genuinely needed to be freed from. And it was the low-self-esteem-driven doctrines that I had to unlearn. Even "grace" was disguised well in her pretty blanket of not-enoughness. You know… a God "loves and accepts me even though I don't deserve His mercy," bla, bla, bla… Even today's more modern, upgraded "grace message" (if we really look deep into it) is all about how a God gives us all what we really don't deserve. I'm sorry, but....yuk! If we follow that premise all the way to its illogical foundations, it is still, once again, all about us not being enough... hence the perceived "need" for "God's grace and mercy" for our not-enoughness.

Interestingly, many from the new, popular Grace Movement are now finally admitting that the Old Testament God of the Bible is not a true representation of the actual God, but rather the self-projected concepts of ancient Jews. They are now selling a "more Christ-like God" to their parishioners. Although I applaud them for coming to their senses about a God who sends bears out of the woods to tear apart little children (2 Kings 2: 23-25), they are probably unaware that this new, upgraded God will cause all sorts of exegetical problems about a (bible-based) God who is what they want him to be in whatever verses they choose that reflects their new "Christ-like God," while flippantly ignoring the hundreds of other verses that, well... not so much. But ... progress is progress.

Our taught need for acceptance

(An excerpt from The Burst of Thunder in Your Ear)

> Recently a man told me that he was struggling with low self-esteem until he finally realized just how much God loved him and accepted him for who he is. He said, and I quote, "I have come to realize that the only constant opinion about me comes from my heavenly Daddy. Since I now understand God's love, I can love others because it is not really me loving them, but Christ (Jesus) loving them through me."
>
> Two things... 1. This man's statement is really not about love, but acceptance. 2. His statement ends with a philosophy I know all too well having been raised in the church, the belief that I am incapable of loving my neighbor as myself on my own. Therefore the only hope for such a dilemma was to be "used" as a sort of host wherein a cosmic Jesus-spirit could "love my neighbor through me." And why

on earth wouldn't a God accept us? Again, saying that "God loves me for who I am" is not a statement about love at all, but about a perceived NEED for acceptance... a need that was sold to us by religion. And the only reason there would even be a conversation about acceptance is if by being born a human rather than a deer there is a possibility of one somehow being ... guilty of something, or rendered UNacceptable, or in some dire need for a God to accept them. I accept all deer as being okay, so why wouldn't a God accept me in the same simple fashion? There's a reason why the church doesn't encourage thinking like this. According to Christian doctrine, something did "have to be done" in order for us to be accepted as (legally) "enough" by a God. And before that (needed) event – in "God's eyes" we were supposedly not enough... not clean enough, not beautiful enough, not innocent enough, not good enough, and not acceptable enough. You know... "undeserved favor." Translation: Favor that we don't deserve. But if that is the true definition of "grace," then I will politely pass.

The Grace Movement (rightfully) leads away from Christianity

(An excerpt from The Burst of Thunder in Your Ear)

"Grace," and yes, even "God's unconditional love" ARE legal terms. According to the Bible, oh yes, they are, and I will explain... but some in the grace movement are attempting to make them something else. That's more than okay with me, but I'm not sure they see where they are headed. When we completely change the biblical meanings of terms like "grace" and "redemption" and "Savior" and even the church's long-held doctrines surrounding the crucifixion, it is just a matter of time for brutal honesty of where that leads. Turning the Judge into a Jolly ole soul is fine with me, but not with mainstream Christianity...

Once you remove the LEGAL out of Christianity the entire thing is destined to implode, and I do mean the entire thing, because mainstream Christianity at its very foundational core is a very legal, judicial-based religion with a very legal, judicial-based God. To deny this is to literally disagree with virtually every denomination headquarters in the land, not to mention the apostle Paul himself who said we must still "present ourselves" to God.

The God of most evangelical Christian churches is a God with a very legal-based relationship with humankind. Some call this "undeserved favor." Please, someone, anyone, answer this… Why would we need to be "accepted" by a God? That's easy… Again; we would have to have first been UNacceptable for some reason to this same God - Who supposedly now "accepts" us for some (legal) reason. Hence the common saying, "Papa God loves and accepts me for who I am." But again, why wouldn't He? And why would we even need to be accepted or loved by a God? Why is that a need for us? Isn't it indeed a taught need?

I understand that some in the grace camp have rewritten the script, turning "original sin" into "original innocence," and that we have always been enough and always accepted by God, but just didn't know it or couldn't see it because of Adam's curse, etc. I also understand that they have turned the crucifixion into (basically) a God Who morphs Himself into a human embryo – only to eventually commit-suicide-via-Roman-death-squad to show us how much He really loves us, rather than a "payment" story. Recently I spent about a week conversing back and forth with a well-known grace preacher about the subject of "grace." He and a couple of his friends spent the first couple of days just making romantic statements and declarations about the beauties of their belief system. They all claimed that they were not "religious," and some of them didn't even like to be categorized as "Christians." But after a week of asking them specifics of what they believed about what Jesus did, and exactly what that achieved for them, I got the answer... And the answer is.......... by dying and then being raised from the dead, Jesus somehow ... secured the "OPTION" for us to obtain (through certain belief protocols – that we hear about from preachers) "eternal life," which is an actual time-based living-forever-in-outer-space-with-Jesus-and-God type of thing... maybe... We think... And that is just how ... fluid the beliefs of so many are... "maybe... I think..."

Another "grace teacher," after calling us modern-day Americans "Gentiles," defined grace as "the kindness of God." My question to him was, "Is this ... 'kindness of God' activated for some but not for others? Couldn't we just live and enjoy life? Wouldn't that be enough? If not, why not? His answer... "Yes, Ken, that might be enough in this life, but the grace of God also promises an enjoyable life for all of humanity in the life to come after this one." If every human gets to "live forever" after their body dies, I may be able to sign onto this, but that is NOT what people like this are saying. There IS a condition and a belief-based protocol one must follow in order to actually obtain this ... "gift" of eternal life.

And what will be the next newly-revealed doctrine that gets upgraded and retranslated? Could it even possibly be that the latest version of the grace message will reach its expiration date, and like many other concepts before it, end up being walked away from for yet another upgrade? Is this ... grace even necessary? Is it magical in nature? Or is it just another hopefully-comforting concept based on ancient scriptures of how we can manufacture doctrines that make us feel significant about ourselves? Regardless of how many different doctrines we employ for the sake of our own self-esteem and view of ourselves, if it is scripture-based it always tends to be a "solution" for something dark that the same scriptures created in the first place. Example: The scriptures offer us a seemingly insurmountable problem, then they offer a solution for the problem they first offered. And no matter how romantic one paints the "solution," it is still being sold by the same source that created the problem in the first place. In some circles they call this "politics."

Bottom line... You cannot base your life philosophy on the Christian Bible and have it turn into something other than Christianity. You cannot take the legalism out of Christianity and still call it Christianity. But so many grace preachers believe they can simply by romancing words like "grace" and "freedom" and "unconditional love" and "Daddy" and "Papa," etc. The doctrines they are twisting into something more palatable will eventually snap back to their original shape and size, because in spite of the positive things about that faith, Christianity remains a legal-based religion which operates by quite stringent faith-based, repentance-based procedures and protocols. The only way around this is lying to ourselves.

The Uninformed Billions

Up until the 1500's there was no such thing as a Bible for the vast majority of Earth's population. I still can't wrap my head around why a God (Who supposedly wishes that no man perish without the option of obtaining eternal life) found it so UNimportant to get that grace message out to the billions of people living between the first and fourteenth centuries in so many cultures and continents around the globe – literally billions who never heard of a man named Jesus, nor the gospel that would supposedly offer them this option of eternal life. Just think for a moment about a thousand years of Native Americans who lived and died here without ever once hearing even a whisper of such things. How many generations is that? And wouldn't this uncomfortable fact matter?

No one "took your place"

When more and more people begin to wake up to the fact that Jesus didn't "take their place" on a cross the shift is going to hit the fan. That hour, I sincerely believe, is approaching much faster than I had first imagined. Nothing has to be done on our part, and nothing ever had to be done on someone else's part in order for you and I to be "enough," or even for you and I to realize that we are enough. Nor is there some sort of mandatory protocol wherein you have to "accept" something or someOne outside of yourself in order to avoid ending up in court after your body dies or as an eternal-life insurance policy. In my honest belief, the taught need to want to be accepted by a God is one of the greatest bags of rocks placed on people's shoulders ever administered by religion. It was totally unnecessary and even damaging... all for the purpose of comfort.

Christianity: Some people want out and in at the same time, and it cannot be done. You cannot turn Christianity into a philosophy. It is a very legal-based religion, not an unconditional-love-based philosophy.

I don't need to be loved and accepted by a God in order to feel good about myself or to feel significant as a human being. This very legal-based (taught) need has nothing to do with love. Again, there's only one reason why we would even feel the need to be accepted by a God - and that reason is the (taught) belief that we were at one point UNacceptable and UNlovable. And that's, well, just dark and twisted in my personal view now.

All this time the whole religiously-packaged "God-is-love" thing was but romantic-sounding poetry with all sorts of procedures, protocols, judgments, and legal ramifications - because of the way it was sold. That verse probably should have been written "LOVE-is-God." I think that would be more accurate, because LOVE is everything. Perhaps it actually IS "all we need."

But the "problem" with LOVE is that it is not about judgment or any of the legal-based not-enoughness doctrines we were so authoritatively taught about ourselves. That's probably the big reason why "LOVE" and "religion" just don't sound quite right in the same sentence to me anymore...

What if the truth about us is that we were born enough? What if we are amazing beyond human description? What if we were indeed born innocent, with absolutely no need for some sort of legal absolution for being born a human? Is that even a possibility?

Honesty about "the fall"

(excerpt from *The Burst of Thunder in Your Ear*)

"Fallen State" (the real foundation of the Christian faith) Let's talk about the foundation of the Christian faith (which - if we are downright honest with ourselves, is not Jesus, but Adam)... God supposedly scooped up some dust from a valley somewhere in the Middle of Iraq, blew His breath into it, making a man (belly button or not). Then after putting Adam into a deep (anesthesiology) sleep, took out one of his ribs and from that rib created a woman. But why is it that a God who can use mere dust to instantaneously create the millions of biological systems necessary for a fully-functional human man, would need to do surgery in order to create a human female? By the way, the belief of the woman having come from the man's rib is clearly the main reason the apostle Paul gave for why women should keep their mouths shut while in a church service (look it up: 1 Timothy 2:13).

Nevertheless, when Adam disobeyed God by sinking his teeth into a piece of fruit, not only was he and his naked girlfriend cursed as well as the ground itself, but the spiritual dna, shall we say, of every human being born after that point would be plagued with some sort of curse. All humans ever born after this point would be born basically infected by this curse, and thus born incomplete, flawed, broken, and separated from God in some sort of ... "fallen" sinful state, needing to be fixed, bought back, ransomed, and "saved" from God's wrath and our fallen, sinful, supposedly-inherited Adamic, disobedient nature. Just a bit mythological? Can we be honest enough to say "yes"?

The story of Icarus (is not true)

Can we tell the difference between legend and reality?

There never was a "fall" of mankind, nor some ... voodoo-like spell that somehow infected all of humankind. That is quite literally what was left over from someone else's ancient Middle Eastern nomadic campfire stories. And I honestly think our hearts have always known this. If the story of Icarus and the melted wax on his wings were in the Bible, I think many grown adults would believe that too. This is a troubling reality. When will we finally be free to think for ourselves?

> *"We thought we had the answers.*
> *It was the questions we had wrong."*
> *- Bono*

Seven

THE TRUTH ABOUT US

Here is someone's response to my position on the majority of humanity being basically good at their core… A man named Chris wrote this… "We are a sinful, depraved people, and without God, His Spirit, and His Word we would completely destroy each other."

But is that what the facts out here on the ground show?

What Humanity Does Best…

(Excerpt from Rebuilding The Village)

> The vast majority of our 7+billion population are instinctively living according to their good nature. An extremely slim minority are responsible for all the crime, disharmony, and suffering in the world. Even the most casual observer of reality can see that most people indeed ARE "basically good" at their core. This is not what the church teaches, but I'll just be one of those who are honest enough to say it – the church is wrong about humanity. And so is "the news."

In my third book, *Rebuilding The Village*, we discuss how the news media paints a bleak picture of humanity by showcasing mostly the negative actions of a very few, and then selling it all as "What on earth is happening to our world!?" The broad-brush picture of "the world" the news and the church tries to sell to us is not an accurate portrayal of what the vast majority of us humans are all about. What the actual data vividly shows is that the vast majority of all humans are respectable, law-abiding, benevolent, caring, nurturing, compassionate-toward-others people. And this does not change because of culture or country. I'm actually going to say it out loud… The teaching that we were all born "basically bad" (because of some ancient, magical curse) is flat out not true. It is not true. That is not what observable reality reveals about us.

It is so unfortunate to hear those who are continually promoting the religion-based philosophy of mankind being incomplete, broken, or in need of some sort of … magical regeneration before they can be effective in bringing any valuable level of help to their neighbors and the world. That is not the humanity I have witnessed. Although a very small minority of the population takes to criminal or abusive activity, the vast majority of humanity has proven to be kind, and courteous.

I remember anytime a crime was committed or someone did something tragically selfish – a member of the clergy would remind us all that the "natural man" instinctively does these unsavory things because it comes "natural" to them. Again, this is factually incorrect. In most cases where heinous crimes have been perpetrated there is almost always a sad history of unfortunate events or a succession of negative choices for the criminal that led up to the crime. Which is to say – most heinous criminal acts are the end result of a life gone horribly and unnaturally downward. Even something as simple as a high school fist fight is something both parties have to "work themselves up" into such a level of violence. It DOESN'T come "naturally," because there's nothing natural about it. What actually comes more natural, and in greater numbers – is people trying to work out their differences and disputes so they don't turn into a fight. Do I really have to give more examples? If we can be honest with ourselves about this, we can all clearly see that most people ARE "basically good."

If it was "natural" for non-religious folks to commit murder, then why do 99.9 percent of our population view such acts as unacceptable, cruel, inhumane, and indeed unnatural? If it is "natural" for non-Christians to disrespect authority, then why is my neighborhood literally FULL of respectful, law-abiding citizens who never go to church? In our community when we lose electricity for three days it is not uncommon to hear a knock on the door from concerned neighbors asking if we are alright. When you tell people you have a terrible cold, the majority of people don't say, "I don't care." They say, "I hope you're feeling better soon." MOST of the public are good people who care about total strangers. It is the very slim minority of the population who are not mindful of others...

When a natural disaster sweeps through a community people naturally step up and say, "What can I do to help?" Again, a very slim minority of that population takes selfish advantage of the situation by breaking into homes and stealing things during a natural disaster. Why don't the majority do the same? Answer: it doesn't come naturally. We all KNOW this to be true, but have been taught differently.

What the vast majority of humanity does best is to behave themselves in the movie theater, at the post office, in the airport, patiently waiting in line at the grocery store, and respectfully filing out of an arena after a rock concert. Another thing humanity does best is lend a hand when others are in need, give money and time for charitable causes, discover and create cures for terrible diseases, build handicap-assessable public amenities for those less fortunate, write new laws that are based on compassion and equality, offer assistance to those in need, and give encouragement to people who are down. Anyone who believes a particular religious group has a corner on compassion and morality simply hasn't thought humanity through completely.

It took me a long time to finally concede to these facts about humanity - because I myself was one of those doctrinally-brainwashed people who used to hear "worldly people" speak from their hearts, saying that "most people are born basically good." I was the one immediately correcting them - as I quoted scriptures and my church's position on how we were all born sinners, etc... also throwing out that ancient verse about our "hearts being wicked"... hence they cannot be trusted. But in reality there's no such thing as "sin," because "sin" is actually an ancient Jewish LEGAL term having to do some ancient religion's belief that a God had rules and particular laws... But "LOVE" has no such thing... and "God" is supposedly "love"...? What?

There is not a cosmic out-there-somewhere JUDGE. All there is - is choices of how to live... We all *were* born "basically good," just like all those outside-the-church people always said from their (UNindoctrinated) hearts. It is all about LIFE and LOVE (for they are one in the same). This may be new to you. This may be different to you. But I really believe that when truth is spoken, however uncomfortable it may be, our hearts resonate with it as being true.

It is (actually) natural for us to help each other.
It is NOT natural for us to hurt each other.

It is (actually) natural for us to care.
It is NOT natural for us not to care.

It is (actually) natural for us to love.
It is NOT natural for us to hate.

It is (actually) natural for us to unite and accept our differences.
It is NOT natural for us to divide and build walls between ourselves.

I grew up being taught just the opposite. Therefore, I grew up being taught a lie about humanity. But we were not "born bad" with the opportunity or choice to one day "become good." It's just the opposite.

Acting Out from who we were told we are...

(Excerpt from The Burst of Thunder in Your Ear)

A very sobering truth is that religion is guilty for a large part of the dysfunction in humanity. What!!!? Yes, religion, including Christianity, and the quite separatist doctrines they teach, ARE to blame for so much dysfunction in society... Staying humble at any cost, including the self-crucifixion of our own healthy self-worth is not true humility at all. It is not noble, not spiritual, not admirable, not enlightening, and definitely not required. And the fear of never quite being enough for a God leads to unhealthy insecurity. It also leads to all sorts of dysfunctional actions and choices – which often lead to suffering for ourselves and others. Because of such religion-driven self-loathing, self-distrusting teachings – millions of people are walking around with low-self-esteem… and thus acting out from those toxic, fear-based, guilt-and-shame-based insecurities, in an "us and them" (judgmental) fashion. And in many cases causing people to be in a perpetual war (believe it or not) with themselves… convinced that they must "die to themselves"... and must "decrease so that Jesus increases" in their lives. Little do they know that this is in fact an incredibly unhealthy and damaging philosophy that results in confusion and dysfunction, not maturity or an abundant life of personal potential and light. What's worse is that this same (taught) mindset gets passed down to their children, building yet more impenetrable walls of dysfunctional relationships and dampening the light in their offspring's lives. Because of their awfully-skewed self-view, this eventually results in other cultural dysfunctions such as crime and even war. And yes, I just did say that.

And all the Christian contemporary songs on the radio make the crucifixion story sound so ... sweet, pleasant, and spiritually romantic. And yet in reality, if we are brutally honest, it is beyond bizarre, gruesome, irrational, unreasonable, illogical, and just a little bit insane.

Since we have inherited (or adopted) that taught sacrificial system we feel dirty, guilty, unworthy, unlovable, and even criminal (very much different than how a deer feels about himself... guilt-free). This is not something we were born with, because we were born innocent, just like the deer. Our need, and almost unhealthy obsession for acceptance and absolution for basically being born a human - was taught to us, and is anything but natural, and anything but true. If we really look deep into the psychology of society we find that people do act out from who they think they are. Whether it is religious fanaticism-driven violence, or drugs-and-alcohol-driven or mental illness-driven, they are all results of how people view themselves and others who are not like them... (separation).

The underlying psychological effects of religion are indeed a contributing factor in what is holding us back from social and cultural progress as a collective civilization. Because of a strong, corporate belief that we are born rebellious, sinful, incomplete, unworthy, in a world that is an "us and them" battlefield, we naturally act out that very incorrect role. I think it would be hard to argue that much of humanity's low self-image is directly connected to incorrect beliefs about ourselves as taught to us by centuries of religious culture. In short, as long as there is religion there will always be financially-rewarding positions in the professional counseling industry. Too strong of a statement? I think not, but perhaps – too honest… too accurate.

Truth will always bring sadness to some and liberation to others. I think one of the main keys is brutal personal honesty about observable reality.

Eight

IS LOVE REALLY "ALL WE NEED"?

"All I need is the air that I breathe and to love you."
— The Hollies

Honesty about "love"

Love isn't all of what it has been cracked up to be. It is actually more... It is actually deeper, wider, simpler, and larger than we ever dreamed it was.

"Love is not subject to some religious law,
so there is no judgment or condemnation in Love.
The verses in Corinthians are describing the nature of Love.
It is our very essence.....our being.
It is the Source that we came from and how we
are connected to all of the Universe. Love is all there is and in
all there is,

expressed as a multi-faceted stone which is One but part of the Whole."

- Shell Gray, Supply, North Carolina

My friend June says, "If God is Love and God is all there is, then we are Love. The only problem with that is that many of us have not become conscious of who we truly are."

I am "love"?

WHAT?

My valued friend Bruce Harbert, from Taylorsville, North Carolina wrote this to me...

"Ken, one thing that really helped me realize the truth of who I am - was by comparing and contrasting what I understood about the concept I was taught of a God... and what I knew and had experienced about Love. From the perspective of a human being... a God is always something outside, separate, and above you. This God is always connected with judgment and causes the one who believes in him to tremble in fear. Love on the other hand, which can be compared to a fathers love, is completely different. This Love is a life-giving Spirit... it is the very life within you. This Love, unlike 'God,' doesn't seek to be worshiped. It will worship you and lift you up. This Love understands it brought you into being by giving you its very life within. Love knows you as itself whereas a God might give you 'grace' and 'mercy'... but you will always be subservient to it... never its equal... never the same... always separate.

Love will lift you up above itself... and desires that you understand and come into your own, not being needy of it but becoming self-sufficient... just as any good father would hope of his child... proud to see them mature and come into their own. Of course in the Christian Bible Jesus' God 'forsook' him... but his real father never did.

Try to understanding this through the eyes of Love... we understand that a man with a God is double-minded and unstable in all his ways... because he hasn't matured in his love...proof being his continuing desire to be God over others (even just with doctrine and theology) and over circumstances in his life and not being able to rest in his own true love. Compare the desire to be God - which is trying to be in control vs. resting in your own love which is giving up all control. When such a man is ready to mature in his love... his God forsakes him... that is to say... he realizes his desire to control others and circumstances around him isn't working for him. This forces him to look WITHIN for the love he seeks, and therein is the final journey of every lost soul... coming home... within... to discover his father in heaven... his eternal life... the love he sought and thought was outside of him... now understood to be his own very being... LOVE... The life-giving Spirit that is all and in all...

And to answer 'how are we love'? We are love by knowing that as our eternal identity that is all and in all... by knowing that 'other' that looks like an 'other' really isn't... but only a part of us that we haven't gotten to know yet. Be careful to entertain strangers... because behind the veil of flesh... they're the self-same Spirit of Love that YOU are... We are ALREADY enough. We know as we are known... and the more you get to know someone... by the Spirit of Love...the more you bear witness of yourself in another."

Thank you, Bruce. Wow!

I was so intrigued by these few paragraphs from Bruce, so I asked several other people to give more feedback on this line of thinking. I see this "love" and "LIFE" as one in the same.

> *"Look at how little children treat each other. Love is the human default position. We learn to hate from those around us who hate."*
> *- Jim High*

*"Love is our nature, innate, who we are,
and hate is something we learned.
Learned behavior .....attitudes."
- Flora Samuel, Miramar, Florida*

*"When I feel love I feel warm,
beautiful, positive emotions and a true sense of freedom.
If I let hate slip in... even for a moment I literally feel sick."
- Sharon Cross Kelch, Cinnaminson, New Jersey*

*"Indoctrination has made us fearful
but the antidote is the remembrance of the Love we are.
We must look within to see the true self and then believe it."
- Shell Gray*

*"There is no 'wanting' in love, and giving is a natural effect."
- John Willox, Seattle*

*"The very essence/nature of our Source...IS Love.
As the branch IS the tree, and the wave IS the ocean...
our very essence IS...Love...as we came from Love,
and are never separated from our Source, except in our mind.
Whatever we want to call IT...there is only One...Source...of which we are ALL...OF.
I don't understand everything...but I do know this.
- Sharon Palmer Tucker*

I love what my friend Sharon Cross Kelch had to say after reading all of this... "Love is everything, it surrounds us, it engulfs us...it *is* us. Through my journey I have found that once we are able to give up control and attachments we reach a new level of love. It's as if we have been washed clean and a whole new feeling of joy fills the cracks in the spirit and the soul and you want to share this love with everyone. There is a gentle calm and a tender feeling of peacefulness that surrounds you and engulfs you, it feels as though you are being held and cradled like a new born babe. It's a familiar feeling... you just know in your heart you have been here or felt this very same feeling before.

I have found as I meet new people there tends to be a whole new level of wonder, curiosity... a welcoming... like never before. And those you have known you want to know better, you want to share your joy and your love. If they are not receptive or responsive to you...that's okay... they're just not where you are at this point in time... maybe they'll get there someday... maybe they won't... no need or reason to control anymore. There really never was any reason to control... we just thought there was... There's just so much freedom in love and it's so beautiful."

Patrick Strickland, from Cleveland, Tennessee says, "What a blessed truth, knowing oneself as Love. A Love that never fell from its place in glory... a timeless Love that is all, in all, as all."

Are the deer and the eagle and the butterfly and the whale "enough" just as they are? If they are, then why wouldn't we be?

Melissa Campbell, from Pittsburgh, Pennsylvania says, "Yep. This describes how it has been in my experience... the putting behind us childish things and moving on into maturity and oneness in truth and love. The greatest of these is love! For years I had a prayer resonating in my spirit for eyes and ears to see and hear. And the answer would echo, 'Who shall separate you from the love of God?' In the wrestling I realized there was no separation between me and 'Thee.' At that point I had to let go of the God I had created and worshipped from afar. It was extremely painful. I went through stages similar to someone in the process of dying... fear, anger, grief, etc. But then... the most incredible release and peace. It felt like a new birth, or death and resurrection... this age of coming into our own."

My friend Murrell says, "I never was able to care for others with a God in my life...there was always a disconnect... I could never feel connected to others the way I felt deep down that I wanted to be or really was. Fear was a factor, and if you weren't of the religious clan that I was part of, well, too bad... just being honest... it was taught to be separate...but now awakening to who I am has consumed the disconnect that was only of the mind...that being religion, God and all that goes with it...which was quite a lot...Knowing myself as All others...I know now that we are the same Spirit...though we may look different and have different jobs, they are all outward things... Pure Love is the only answer... because a God picks and chooses who to care for and who not to...Love is not God and has no need of a God. For Love only knows Itself in All as All."

Frank Johnson, a man I consider a valuable life mentor, said this, "Our human capacity to love is first learned; it can be given or withheld based on our experience of life. But, what is unknown to us is the Source of that love. Love is the very essence of Life which is far greater and deeper than our mind's ability to perceive. That is, until we are willing to let go. The self, our ego identity, stands firm like a dam, restricting the natural flow of love. Love can be likened to a river that flows through us without effort and without end. In truth, we are Love."

Words from a religious skeptic

Skepticism doesn't only come from outside the doors of the church. Here is someone's doubting response to what all my friends just shared... They said, "Ken, what is really scary to me is that a lot of these friends of yours actually believe the nonsense they are saying." This caused me to sit back in my chair a bit and think to myself... "What exactly is there to be afraid of, unless of course we *do* end up in court after we die – on trial for being born a human rather than a deer."

Honesty about "LOVE"
Is "God" really "love"?
Is "love" really "God"?
Or is love just "love"?

Is "God" simply a hopeful, anthropomorphic explanation of ancient men about how the universe operates? The thing is... if God is love, then why doesn't the God of the Bible accurately portray all the characteristics of the Bible's own definitions of love? Does love judge? Is love vengeful? Does love require payment or devotional adherence? Does it keep a record of the wrong others have done, or even keep track of your beliefs? Does love grow weary of patience or tolerance? Does love change its mind? Because the Bible shows the God of Abraham, Isaac, and Jacob doing ALL of these things.

If we try real hard, with the help of some crafty scholars, can we perhaps romanticize and poeticize these discrepancies away as if they are not real problems?

I get by with a little help from my friends

Part of me wants to write this entire book by myself, with no feedback from anyone, you know... so I can take full credit as the "author"... but that wouldn't be accurate at all. In fact, without the wonderful people I am about to introduce to you, this book would have never happened...

> *Most of our wisdom comes from*
> *a thousand different people,*
> *so paying only one will only take you*
> *as far as that one has gone.*

One of my friends, Diana Robbins said this... "The only 'god' I know is Love, not a person, not a 'Lord,' not a law-giver, not a ruler, but a substance, a force, an intelligent Presence that is in us all, AS us all. Sadly, this Love that we are often goes unexpressed due to mental conditioning and teachings of religion. This ground of being that I call Love bears little or no resemblance to the 'god' I've heard preached from many pulpits, the monstrous and bloodthirsty vengeful and jealous God of the Israelites. However, I believe that Jesus of Nazareth knew this Love, called It Father, and knew that he and we are ONE with it at the core of our being. Quantum physics, via the holographic model of the universe, with its understanding of the all in one and one in all, micro-cosmically and macro-cosmically, bears out this understanding of 'God' as ALL there is. I call It Love because I cannot perceive of this Source of All being anything but beneficent. There are so many, many wolves in sheep's' clothing walking around pretending to represent this 'personal' and demanding, rule-setting God, having forgotten there is only the ONE expressed as many. I'm not drinking their Kool-Aid."

My friend Bruce Harbert had this to say… "And if you know this… you like Jesus can say… without reservation… 'If you've seen me you've seen the father'… yet…'my father is greater than I' (my own individual being) because the Love I know I AM is all and in all. Our inherited concept of 'God' is just who we thought we were…before we took our inward journey and realized our eternal life… Love."

Same yesterday, today, and forever?

If "God" is the "same yesterday, today, and forever," then either God is not these things, or the entire Bible is not inerrant… and not all completely true… full of many not-so-enlightened writers and a few very enlightened ones.

So what really is God? Perhaps "God" actually is just a hopeful Zeus-like explanation of the mysterious, yet-to-be-fully-understood operational dynamics of the universe/nature. But is that too scary? Too … out-of-the-box uncomfortable? If so, why? Scientists and forward thinkers of today work from their own 'point of perception,' it is true, but they are more willing than ancient religious men to change their minds when new evidence that births new scientific paradigms become obvious. Religion and its comfort-based thinking has nothing to do with this.

I'm no longer an avid reader of the Bible, but I do love what my friend Robert Rutherford, from Eatonton, Georgia said… "The Bible is a collection of writings by ancient, Middle Eastern Jewish men, steeped in the fables, history and doctrines of the Jewish culture and faith, and the God portrayed in those old religious writings is a view of a God through the branches of the tree of the knowledge of good and evil - in the shadows of Judaism. John the Apostle was a Jew. His view of God was Jewish, in the beginning. He was a SON OF THUNDER! His suggestion to 'CALL DOWN FIRE FROM HEAVEN' on those who believed differently was in 'GOD-LIKE' fashion, yet Jesus had a different perspective, very much unlike the God of the Jews. Jesus clearly opposed the Bible of their day and openly disobeyed it time and time again. He even brought up scripture given by Moses, their hero, and showed why it was wrong for those who would now be led by the Spirit. After a few years with Jesus, John's tune changed. At the end of his ministry he is no longer trying to call down fire. He has concluded: God is love. Everyone that loves is born of God and knows God.' The 'God of the Bible' is not the REA DEAL. LOVE is the REAL DEAL."

"IF YOU CAN'T TRUST YOURSELF, WHO CAN YOU TRUST?"

(by Dan Pederson)

"In Christian fundamentalism you are taught to distrust yourself. Instead of trusting yourself, you are taught to trust someone else. In particular, you are taught to trust your pastor and dozens of people who lived thousands of years ago (some of whom never revealed their identity). In other words, you can't use your own judgement, because it can't be trusted. But you can use it to trust the judgement of others, even people you've never met. There is no lack of irony in this. Nobody ever seems to wonder how it is that they can even recognize the truth by listening to a preacher or reading the Bible if they can't even trust their own judgement in the first place. If you can fool yourself, others can fool you too. And if you are capable of recognizing truth in the words of others, you are also therefore capable of recognizing it in yourself.

Some people act like God himself wrote the Bible. This belief exists because people want to be lead. We want life to be laid out in black and white. It makes us feel better. We don't want to grapple with the uncertainties of life. It makes us feel insecure. We want something we can anchor ourselves with. But the Bible was not written by God. It's possible, and likely, that parts of it were written under inspiration. But the Bible is not one book, it is many books containing many truths and falsehoods. You have to sort it out in your own heart and through education. This is how you learn truth. If we insist that the entire Bible is literally true and inspired, then we will remain in ignorance and believe a lot of foolish things.

When we read the Bible there is a tendency to believe that it is speaking to us directly, but in reality the various books and letters in the Bible were written to specific people living thousands of years ago, in a culture alien to our own. The Bible should be read in that context. The Bible is not as authoritative as your church or favorite preacher wants you to believe. In many cases, they mean well, but are mistaken. In other cases, it's in their best interest for you to believe in the absolute authority of the Bible (and the preacher as its messenger). It is useful in giving them authority and influence over you.

'Holy Scripture' is only holy insofar as someone says that it's holy. And it's only the final word until someone comes along and says it's not. Jesus himself contradicted scripture. Jesus and the early Christians came along and totally disrupted what the Jews had been taught from the Torah (Old Testament). And right from the beginning, no Christians could totally agree about what it meant to be a follower of Christ. Even the two leaders, Peter and Paul did not totally agree, and today Christians are more divided than ever.

If you believe what you read in the Bible, it will become real for you. The true parts and the untrue parts. Find out what is true and what isn't, otherwise you might be better off without it. There are many people who would have been. It would have been better for the Crusaders to have never known about it. That is, better for their victims.

You don't have to believe something just because someone with a confident voice says so. Let them present you with the evidence that what they are saying is true. And read the works of professional historians and real biblical scholars who have provided evidence that much of what is taught in church is not true. Listen to both sides before making a judgment.

We tend to go looking for God outside of ourselves. But God is within. God is found in peaceful moments, and rarely if ever through the words of fiery preachers. What the fiery preacher gives you is not God. The fiery preacher excites your emotions, but does not lead you to the quiet inner presence of God.

There is no evidence that Jesus' sermons were loud and emotionally charged. Don't make excuses to yourself for why the preacher's words or tone are not consistent with the Bible. And don't make excuses to yourself for why the Bible is inconsistent with itself. If you are noticing inconsistencies, you are discovering truth." (Dan Pederson: livingwithconfidence.net)

Love is God = "Idolatry"?

A devout evangelical Christian recently told me, "Ken, to say that 'God is love' is correct, but to say 'Love is God' is idolatry."

But I just can't imagine the ancient God of the Jews saying, "Thou shalt have no other gods before Me, INCLUDING LOVE!!!" I think this whole ... "idolatry" thing is just one more sad example of the very legal-based God that the ancient Jews "served," and in a quite legal-based construct. A reward-and-punishment God is truly not "Love" at all, and never was.

My friend John says, "Are we ready to really consider the energetic aspect of 'divinity' and the 'causative formation' aspects of the energy that pervades everything, the universe, each cell of our bodies, the hearts and minds of all? Really? This is where I get the most kickback and argument... 'It's eastern philosophy,' or 'it's not in the Bible,' or (and my favorite), 'you elevate yourself above the Word'... And yes, I do elevate myself above the written accounts of ancient humans, living in a paradigm of fear and separation. These men desperately had to categorize and explain the natural phenomena of the word as in total control by an external deity... when actually there is no control. The heart knows this instinctively, the mind [attempts to] blocks this with a vengeance."

John, attempting to clarify the essence of what he said, added this... "Our concepts of the divine have all too often been of an anthropomorphic nature - there is only one eternal truth and we are it... Hard to take for many, but it does seem this simple, and the comfort-based resistance is still large. This, if taken and really looked at, requires personal responsibility for our own thoughts, emotions, and actions... and the image we hail from that is causative to all of it. The energy of the universe, is causative and formative, but has no agenda, and certainly no judgment. The 'laws' of the universe, are wondrous and mysterious, and we have worked with and worked against, but we can rest assured that when we work with, we 'reap' peace, joy, abundance, health... when we work out of phase, we reap turmoil, depression, lack, and sickness. These are not 'judgments,' but just consequence of 'working outside natural law.'

This statement does away mostly with the old Abrahamic concepts that are still believed by many theists - stunting the development of humans for millennia."

In a conversation about our own humanitarian love on social media, a man wrote, "Please don't tell me I can't be a loving person without a God. I have plenty of my own love, and have done heaps of loving, compassionate things for others without the help of a God." A very passionate theist named Chris joined in, wanting to make sure we all realize just how helpless and hopeless we are without a God... He wrote, "Without God there is no love. God was the reason for your loving acts; you just didn't give Him credit for it. Now see... even what you thought was your own love and your own loving acts - you turned it around into you seeking glory for yourself and taking that glory and credit away from God. You see, your good deeds are like filthy rags to Him and you cannot truly love outside His presence. This idea is simply promoting self-glory, not God's glory, and it is not a Christian idea."

But here we go again... Why on earth would it even be necessary to "give a God the credit"? What exactly does that accomplish? And again, if we are honest, this line of indoctrinated thinking stems from the belief that we can make whatever Force brought about 500 billion galaxies happy or sad. Stop for a minute and just think of the arrogance required here. And gently inhaling a warm, tropical breeze is just as amazing to an atheist as it is to a theist who is perpetually saying "Thank You God for the ocean breeze." Actually, the little dude with the funny hat sitting on the beach smoking weed is probably enjoying and appreciating this tropical setting on a deeper, more appreciated level than both of them. But you get the point...

And ... "promoting self-glory"? Let me please ask the question... If we are simply loving and caring for others in a "left-hand-doesn't-know-what-the-right-hand-is-doing" fashion, is that really promoting self-glory? Or is it simply BEING who and what we truly are at our core? Is it really such a crime to finally get to a place in our lives where we actually love ourselves and are able to celebrate our own beauty? What sort of tyrants would teach against such raw innocence?

We sure don't like to admit it, and we will swear it is not true, but "worship" of a deity has always been about "paying" on some deeper, psychologically-undetected level. And it always will be.

Look… step back and really look… This whole "giving God the glory" thing is about comfort. We pay God compliments and He gives us comfort in exchange for the payment. The whole judgmental aspect of this towards "unbelievers" is about an actual belief that God-complimenters are better, or … on some higher life level than atheists, supposedly with more wisdom, more compassion, more insight, more meaning, more purpose, more happiness, more genuine inner peace, and just all around better people. But is that actually true? I think not.

What About Sin?

(excerpt from Field of Grasshoppers)

> The idea of "original sin" came from St. Augustine with his need to make Jesus a second Adam in order to fix the problems with the first one.
>
> Do we still define sin the same as ancient Judaism does? Is it still a legal matter? Is sin an actual long list of activities that are against the Law of Moses, or is it more of a matter of missing the mark? Could it perhaps be more accurately defined as missing the whole point of life itself? My friend, Jen (my editor), put it this way: "Sin is done. Sin is related to Law. What 'law' do we 'sin' against today, and what is the 'penalty' for 'sinning' against that 'law'? The Law of Moses was never given to us in the first place, so we cannot 'sin' against that Law. Jesus came to 'make an end of sin.'"

Recently a man said to me, "Before Jesus, all we had was the Law." I replied, "When exactly did the Capital Hill area of Seattle have the Law of Moses?" I am not a first-century Jew or Gentile. It is beyond amazing how I had somehow been romantically convinced that I was.

Eckhart Tolle refers to this unfortunate state of mankind as dysfunction or even madness. Hinduism calls it maya. Buddhist writings talk of it as dukkha. Christianity calls it the original sin. I love Eckhart's version of this 'missing the mark,' in his book *A New Earth*. He explains it as living unskillfully and blindly, suffering from the consequence and also causing others to suffer.

Perhaps the original sin was not that Adam ate some forbidden fruit, but that at one point man convinced us that we are all naked and should be ashamed of ourselves for the crime of being human. I do find it interesting how secular law has evolved into an 'innocent until proven guilty' system, whereas the church continues to teach 'guilty until proven innocent.'

What About Forgiveness?

(excerpt from Field of Grasshoppers)

Is forgiveness all about a legal or judicial need for 'absolution' so that we are (legally) in 'right standing with God' and thus 'legally eligible' for both blessings and safe passage into the afterlife? Is forgiveness more for our benefit or more for God, as a requirement to somehow gain or regain His favor or appeasement? Isn't 'forgiveness' more about inner peace from releasing our judgments and ill feelings toward others? Is it about acquittal, or more about renewal?

To me, it was beginning to look like religion in general was about two main things: 1. Paying God. 2. Making sure that you have. In religion, it seems like it is your job to make God happy (tall order). It is continually romanced as a heart matter but in reality it is a legal, obligation-based matter that is continually being sold as a 'heart matter.'

A Pantheist's view of "God"

I was absolutely blown away by this very insightful pantheist friend of mine, Poffo Ortiz, who wrote the following commentary on this subject… "Ken, of course the god of the bible is full of contradictions, inconsistencies and seemingly hypocritical actions, attitudes and behaviors… because it was a HUMAN construct. A false concept propagated by less-than-perfect men with social and political agendas, who projected all of their jealously, pettiness, anger, bigotry, violence and discrimination onto a celestial being.

Many are confused about the ultimate origins of love. Suffice to say, it does not come from a transcendent being somewhere 'out there' but from within all higher life forms who've evolved enough to possess the capacity to give, receive and experience love. You could say, 'love comes from God' and you would not be wrong… of course it comes from God, EVERYTHING comes from God. And there's no reason to relegate it to a 'natural evolutionary mechanism' as if that would make it any less extraordinary. To wholeheartedly accept other organisms and respect and care for all Life is the highest action/activity we can do as mammals. And why consider it less of a thing because it is an evolutionary mechanism? Everything is a product of evolution, including our ability and desire to love others. We are social animals, it is true… so loving each other had tremendous survival benefits as our species evolved… but given enough time and the right conditions, this is the path of any highly evolved organism, i.e. to develop morality and display altruism, etc. Not only because it is a common, biological function intended to simply perpetuate the species (although even this in and of itself reveals the intention), but because it is the will of the Omnia to find cohesion and return to singularity by accepting and loving every other differentiated aspect of Itself.

IS LOVE REALLY "ALL WE NEED"?

If you listen carefully to what I've been saying, I've never advocated for a conscious entity. As long as the Universe has existed, no such being has ever been. Only that all of this profundity of Life and order and complexity came about due to a latent programming that is embedded into existence Itself. Not programmed or embedded or designed by something else in a dualistic sense, but latent within the Universe, because it is an eternal quality OF the Universe. Does Nature/the Cosmos/Omnia love us the way Theism's god supposedly loves us? This is really a tremendous question and I think it is one (despite what many Atheists claim) that begs to be asked, especially by Pantheists like myself. Obviously, Nature/the Universe/the Cosmos, does not 'love us' in a personal, individualized, deliberate human way (the way most theists perceive), because Nature is not a person, but a collective, creative force. That being said, I think Nature absolutely does 'loves us' and 'cares for us' in a deeper and even more personal, profound way than we could ever imagine, that is far more complex and individualized and intimate on a certain, incomprehensible level. Just look at our bodies' healing factor, look at the constant regeneration of cells and the tenacious imperative to live and reproduce and thrive. That, IS love.

Renowned evolutionary biologist and outspoken Atheist Richard Dawkins once made this statement: 'The total amount of suffering per year in the natural world is beyond all decent contemplation. During the minute that it takes me to compose this sentence, thousands of animals are being eaten alive, many others are running for their lives, whimpering with fear, others are slowly being devoured from within by rasping parasites, thousands of all kinds are dying of starvation, thirst, and disease. It must be so. If there ever is a time of plenty, this very fact will automatically lead to an increase in the population until the natural state of starvation and misery is restored. In a universe of electrons and selfish genes, blind physical forces and genetic replication, some people are going to get hurt, other people are going to get lucky, and you won't find any rhyme or reason in it, nor any justice. The universe that we observe has precisely the properties we should expect if there is, at bottom, no design, no purpose, no evil, no good, nothing but pitiless indifference.'

Now despite how terrifying and unsettling this is to consider, I have to agree with Dawkins' in his statement, since this is a correct observation of the natural world... but the truth is, at the same exact time, bear cubs and fawns and baby rabbits and adolescent apes are also at this moment, frolicking and playing in the warmth of the sun, or nestling into their burrows and enjoying the pleasures that Mother Earth provides. She is cruel, but she is also kind, and gives us everything we need to sustain ourselves. Life is both harsh and loving, because the Laws of Nature force us to stretch and grow and adapt to become more efficient at everything.

And there is another aspect to this... us.

As expressions of the Divine, the love we feel towards one another and all of life is an evolution and a manifestation of Nature's capacity and potential to love. The highest degree of love that a person could feel for another human or for an animal or the earth IS the Cosmos, loving itself. The closer we come toward singularity, the more this love will find greater expression in the world. Nature has always 'loved us,' as It has always loved Itself, and sought ever and always to perpetuate Its own existence. Its mind has just evolved from the status of pure survival and reproduction and protection of Itself, to a more altruistic, unifying compatibility, through us. It is seeking homeostasis and balance at all times... and WE are the conduit, the medium for that incredible process to unfold. And I'm not just expressing an opinion here, this is an observable fact. How could we have the feelings of love or the pleasures and enjoyments we experience, if Nature did not provide the means for us to do so? Of course we all experience pain and suffering and loss, just as Dawkins' comment demonstrates and it is literally happening at every hour, every second of the day, to both humans and animals, everywhere. And so the answer is, we are at all times experiencing BOTH the cruelty and the love of Nature. And when you understand what that 'harshness' and cruelty does, the effect it has on us as Natural Selection does its job and weeds out the sick and the weak and promotes the strong and the healthy in the natural world, and when you see and understand what Nature has done in allowing us to evolve to become the most successful species on the planet. With massive brains and a cerebral cortex and prefrontal lobe that has this tremendous capacity to love and nurture and care for all Life in a selfless and altruistic way, than I would say the overarching design of it all is intrinsically based on love, because that's what we are moving towards in the evolution of our consciousness as a whole.

Most animals haven't had the time and freedom to evolve as we have that would allow them to develop those higher faculties of reason and imagination and abstract thought (these are all the consequences of being a higher evolved animal). Given enough time, a sheep or a monkey or an owl would be grappling with the same issues. And when I say 'time' I don't just mean linear time, but the opportunities provided if they were more successful as a species in the same capacities that we have been, e.g. developing a prehensile thumb, being bipedal, having a larger brain that allows them to manipulate their environments and build things to aid them with gathering food, etc.

Incidentally, what I am talking about is a very pertinent concept for me, because as an ex-Christian and someone coming out of a belief system where I literally had to grapple with the notion that there was no anthropomorphic deity who loved me and cared about me personally, I had to figure this all out for myself... and my peace and sanity depended on it. And now, as a Pantheist, it's an issue I've wrestled with and been forced to consider for a very long time as well. I'm a very spiritual person, but not in the sense that I believe in supernatural realms or gods and goddesses. I believe what my eyes and ears tell me and what my mind perceives and my intuition senses... and what my heart and soul cries out for and longs for above all else, is a world united in love. Where does that sentiment come from, if not from Nature? Many atheists do not understand this and they see a cold and uncaring Universe that's indifferent to them, but WE are expressions of that Universe, so in my eyes, the greatest thoughts and feelings a person could have, is a perfect reflection of the mind of the Cosmos. Animals feel love and affection, people show love and feel compassion, therefore... Nature loves." (Poffo Ortiz – biopantheism.wordpress.com)

"Nature has always 'loved us,' as It has always loved Itself, and sought ever and always to perpetuate Its own existence."
- Poffo Ortiz

Charlie Edward Shoemaker, from Rochester, New York said this, "I find it interesting that when asked very directly - Jesus described God as 'spirit' and 'Father in spirit.' In first century times, 'spirit' meant something very particular.

It was a definition closer to what 'new agers' and spiritual mystics would describe God the spirit as an intelligent universe but also incomprehensible to quantify. When Jesus refers to God as 'Father,' it is the same as when one talks about God's 'ear' or 'right hand,' God is spirit, not flesh and body. Those references of physical and even gender are for relative purposes from the human perspective, not actual descriptions of God's being. While Jesus may have used the very familiar 'father' to describe the intimacy of spiritual relationship, he didn't mean it in the sense of the male ruler and master, if he used the wording 'father' at all."

Brian Malone, from Novato, California shared this… "All perceivable manifestations of energy (every-thing) arises within the unified field of consciousness … Call it or know it as God, Source, Tao, Brahma, Trinity, Yahweh, Presence, Nirvana, Heaven, Omniscience, Enlightenment… Be still and know that I AM Love as All is Love. Infinite, eternal, boundless, inclusive … LOVE. Though "it" is ineffable, mysterious and seemingly ethereal, the affect/effect that the word love tries to name and describe seems only able to be presented metaphorically."

Thank you, Murrell Copas, for writing this… "Without the Bible would any know of a God… and saying that the Bible does point to our spirit… but many things in nature tell us the same… the God we have all been told about is handed down from generation to generation. The God I was given (probably not the same God you were given) is all about right and wrong or good and evil (Judgment). Love has no need of a God of correction or judgment and has no desire to control any. Once I knew who Love or Spirit is who I am I lost all need of trying to control, judge, religion with all the rules and laws and a God. Love is equal and knows all as Itself. I never knew a God that did."

And from my valued naturalist colleague, Jim High… "For all of human self-conscious history Gods of all kinds have been part of human thinking. This was because as the human animal became self-conscious and aware there was much that they did not understand. The seemingly correct answer was, 'The Gods did it.' Many cultures still have many Gods. Some have only one. Evolution is a very slow process taking tens of thousands (indeed millions) of years. So in one short lifetime of 75 to 100 years we see no evolution or changes, but they are there. In the future there will be no Gods because humans will more completely understand the cycle of life which they themselves live. We don't all evolve at the same rate; therefore a few of us already realize that there are no Gods by any definition people assign to God in their attempts to save the God idea and concept. So without a God what is there you might ask? ... the connection of all life to all other life. We are connected to everything that lives. And we are slowly beginning to understand how important that is to the future of the planet. The future is not 'in God's hands,' there is no God with hands. The future is totally in our hands, and always has been."

And I have personally grown to expect deepness from my friend Dean Dosher, who says, "God ... is just a word... birthed of the mind in its attempt to answer that which it yet understands... love is known of all, desired of all.... it gets trampled on by the "god" of man... in ignorance and by the desire to preserve identity. A God and fear are taught alliance to control or attempt to control what is not 'liked'... Little is really known about love until you begin to submit to its journey, which if completed will take you to the place of all understanding of all things... and that 'God' that your mind birthed will vanish. Love is not simply an emotion. It is not simply a word or some sort of out-there Person or Entity. It's the very foundation of your person, and in it is the truth of all things."

My friend, Kevin Sturges, from Milwaukee, Wisconsin says, "Jesus came to reveal the truth that was not found in the external God they were serving, nor in the religion they had created, but was a truth discovered in the 'kingdom' within oneself. There is also a major difference in the selfish kind of love the world justifies itself in of the flesh and the true selfless unconditional love that is not self-seeking."

My friend David Summers shared these sentiments... "The early imaginations of humankind, just emerging from the Stone Age and only a few centuries after the first appearance of language, hardly consist of 'fact-checked' history. History was changed from generation to generation. Why do we tenaciously cling to just these early stories of biblical characters and events when we don't care to study about where they were, who the non-religious leaders were, how they lived, what the civics of liberal and conservative thoughts of their time period were, as well as other types of influencing societies that existed in neighboring regions? If we continue to equate the thinking of those times with the thinking of our modern-day (and every-day) thinking why are not those ideas, imaginations and histories just as important?

The quick answer is we simply don't... for the most part... except for when it comfortably aligns with our inherited religious concepts. Why? Because we refuse to believe and accept our own intelligence - such as some of the more progressive thoughts on subjects like "God," how the universe actually works, and even entertaining new definitions of what "love" is and how it could have possibly come about. We are an evolved people. We only lose our modernity when we begin to think of life within a totally-imagined prism of ancient Middle Eastern stories, first relayed orally down through generation to generation, then by primitive symbols within religious concepts interpreted by their so-called 'smart' people of the day. The truth is - the ordinary man of ancient times did not think in the same mental concepts and processes as we do today. To compare our level of education, science, and indeed consciousness to these primitive, nomadic tribes AND their 'really smart people' (the prophets) is ludicrous. We are only self-realized modern thinkers when we think as such, not when we try to understand and duplicate the thinking of ancient tribal nomads."

And please listen with concentrated inner honesty to what Wendy Jenkins from Windsor, Ontario has to say... "I'm not convinced that 'God' is Love. I wonder who this God really is when considering... Genesis 1:1 He who was alone in the beginning [Was, Is, Will Be] created the gods [Elohim], the heavens [universe], and the earth. In many places in scripture it speaks of God and the Father, Jesus said that it was God who forsook him. I have read where Jesus said we are to Love God, but I have not read where he says that God loves us, but he does say the Father Loves us... 'and that the world may know that thou hast sent me, and hast loved them, as thou hast loved me.' Are we to believe that 'God' and the 'Father' are one as most believe? I see consistent unconditional Love coming from the Father, but not so from this God. Could this God really be us, our judgement of ourselves and others that we hold in the carnal mind? When we come to realize we are One with the Father and All - this God disappears with the renewed mind."

Suzana Olivier, from Abu Dhabi says that 'God' is a figure of speech for something we cannot yet put into words and accept.

My Colorado friend, Joe Sheader... "Does love exist? Love exists, and I feel with empirical observation that it absolutely is to be found beyond humans into other species. However, as one who does not subscribe to any belief in any god of any kind, the saying 'god is love' or 'love is god' is meaningless to me. I understand the usage as metaphor and if there was to be any god at all I'd hope such be described and expressed love... which would by necessity fundamentally discount the rantings of pretty much all religions. As with morality I feel love is an emergent and wondrous phenomenon of living, relating sentient beings via evolution. I don't think it of any supernatural origin."

David Jewell writes, "The God of the Bible is a construct of primitive mankind. 'He' is the result of an incapable need to hopefully make sense of what was, and was yet, undisclosed."

Pam Boyington Holmes says, "The God of the Bible represents the viewpoints of a particular people at given times in history. It's time to evolve."

My dear mentor and friend Sharon Cross Kelch... "This is what the Bible says, however, I have not experienced this or witnessed this practice by the religious leaders of the churches I have attended: 'Love is patient, love is kind. It does not envy, it does not boast, it is not proud. It does not dishonor others, it is not self-seeking, it is not easily angered, and it keeps no record of wrongs. Love does not delight in evil but rejoices with the truth. It always protects, always trusts, always hopes, and always perseveres. Love never fails. When I was a child, I talked like a child; I thought like a child, I reasoned like a child. When I became a man, I put the ways of childhood behind me... And now these three remain: faith, hope and love. But the greatest of these is love.'

I no longer believe in a 'sky God' and the teachings of a judgmental God who lords over people causing pain and fear. I believe that 'Love is just that... Love.' It does not need a Captain or a kingdom Ruler or a King. I do have faith and hope in the belief that the teachings of religion and all the fear and control tactics that go along with these teachings will fall away and Love will prevail. I do not want or need a God... I have love. And love IS enough."

Roger Winters, from Johnson City, New York says, "I do believe that a 'God' or a 'He' is definitely a man-made concept. His characteristics and personality are clearly humanistic in nature, if we are to believe the stories from the Bible. Love is a human trait that resides in all of us, regardless of culture or religion. The universe has its own way, operates naturally for the preservation of all that is. Man is part of that, as are the trees, ocean, planets, oxygen, reproduction, and all that is. When humans learn to flow with the natural, instead of resisting it, trying to control it, or making up comfort-based alternatives to it, we shall begin to experience and witness harmony among everyone. I think that religion and the emphasis on placing the Bible above all else is a huge roadblock and hindrance to our true growth, as it distracts us from life's realities."

Own your own love, man!

> *"If you didn't care ... what happened to me, and I didn't care ... for you, we would zig zag our way through the boredom and pain, occasionally glancing up through the rain..."*
> *– Roger Waters*

Why do you think you care so much about others? Do you think you have the answer to that question? Do you think it is deep and profound and mystical and "spiritual" or magical in nature, or do you think it is simply who and what you are? I know that some folks have been convinced that they are just not enough to possess such beautiful benevolence, and that some Entity outside of themselves must have had mercy on them, allowing them to love others with some ... higher love that is better than their own humanitarian love. This is more than incorrect, in my honest belief. We don't need a "higher love." That is not a healthy philosophy, but just more ... not-enoughness theology. What we need is a simple comprehension of our own natural humanitarian love, and an appreciation for that same love in others. Add to the fact that your own love is enough, and always was enough, and we are starting to get the picture as it really is.

Loving people actually comes quite natural for most folks. If loving people DOESN'T come naturally for you, some sort of "spiritual regeneration" is not what is needed. I hate to be so frank, but what is needed is professional counseling. Whoever told you that your own natural humanitarian love is not enough to get your neighbor-loving done - was wrong. Likewise, whoever told you that you need a God to love your neighbor *through* you, because your own human love is just not enough - were also wrong. Yes, wrong, incorrect, not true.

People who have a hard time loving people have probably been told that their love just isn't good enough on its own... to the extent that they finally believed it... to the extent that they now live that belief. No wonder they have to *try* to love their neighbor, or ask a God to "love their neighbor through them." If that's you my friend, they set you up to believe inadequacies about yourself and your good nature that are just not true. And since they are not true, you don't have to believe it anymore. That whole ... "you are ugly, but we can help" talk is literally all backwards to the truth about who and what you are.

The real reason you love and care about others is because that is who and what you *are*. Your own beauty is enough, and always has been enough. What's more is that you don't *owe* someone for who you are, or for the beauty of who you are. The only reason you are amazing is because you are amazing. Accept yourself as incredible, and then watch what happens... I think you'll be pleasantly surprised.

More comments from friends

My friend Colin Lagerwall says, "Self-perception has always been flawed by 'another'... Therefore we will never need another 'other' to rectify the truth within us that has always been... We will know the truth about ourselves (and be freed from 'an other's' perspective) regardless from whom the perspective originates."

Murrell Copas writes, "Yes ! We Love simply because It's who We are. The only mystery is thinking you're who and what you've been told you are. But once you realize who you are for yourself, all the mysteries will be uncovered, and you will know Love is really who you have and always will be, and the Love you are will consume all the lies you thought you were. Yes, you are more than enough."

Wendy Jenkins tells us all, "It's sad, because of so much religious teaching I always thought myself to be so unlovable, but inside all I felt to be was Love. Love for not only all other peoples, but all of nature as well. The Love I feel is so powerful that at times I have to look away and swallow hard, it is so overwhelming. I Know that Love is who I am."

Michael Camp, a fellow author from Seattle said, "One problem is the bizarre, Calvinistic theology of the depravity of humankind, which is a lie. Our natural self is at home with loving and caring for others. But if we have not been loved and cared for, or have inherited or been brainwashed with theologies of fear, then we have capacity for lashing out at others. But it's not our natural self, it is a lost self."

Shell Gray... "When you come to realize the divine human that you are it is no longer an action of love to others, it is simply BEing Love. Others sense it and it's not fake because you are the same in all situations. It's as normal to you as breathing. You have to take no thought."

Frank Johnson... "Things appear to go well when we try to love with the mind, that is, until the tide changes. If we have not had a deepening realization of our true Nature - be prepared. When circumstances shift (and they will), we are thrust into confusion. Like the pushing of a button, our emotions surface faster than a lightning strike, and we are instantly caught-up in the drama. By contrast, realizing the Truth of our Being or the Heart of Love within, is to become aware of the reality of who we really are. And that can only effectively take place through a consistent practice of entering within and staying with that inner silence. Spiritual truth learned as a doctrine is but a man-made formula that remains a mere assumption held by the mind. When internalized, what Jesus revealed results in true transformation, which translates to an awareness of who we are and an immediate understanding of the Eternal Life that flows through us."

Jim High wrote… "Love is an emotion and all our emotions come from our millions of years of evolution into the human animal. So it is built in. Sometimes we forget where and how we came to be. I don't care if it is a best friend or someone you just met for the first time. You are quietly talking with them, but if you reach out and hold their hand you feel a deeper connection. That is our built in love at work."

Sharon Palmer Tucker, a retired minister says, "Once the whole premise that we are corrupt, unrighteousness (from infancy) and 'by nature... children of wrath'...has been exposed as the 'Lie' they are...we suddenly realize the valuable quality of our Being. Provided we don't entertain negativity, bitter, unforgiving and darkened 'thoughts'... left to our natural inclination... we are deeply Loving, Compassionate, Forgiving and Caring people... expressing in a myriad of ways, from rushing to pay for the mother who's groceries added up to $8 more than she had (with 3 children clutching her legs)... to being part of a team who delivers food to people in war-torn and destitute countries... to reaching down to pick up a shivering, starving puppy left in the rain... to skillfully bringing hope back into the life of one who has lost all hope for living. It is not something we do, IT'S WHO WE ARE! And the more we get to know who we are... going within... to the stillness of our essence... the more and more beautiful those expressions are. A testament... from whence we sprang... in my estimation. Not a 'without which I can do nothing'... but a 'Me and my Source are One'."

Reine Fox Fisher writes, "I know I'm a person with deep love. I've always loved everyone, even before I knew what love was. It is most definitely who I am. Even for those who some would say are unlovable... I don't have it in me not to love them! I've gone through the retreats; I've heard the whole religious thing of 'give the credit to God,' and that they can't love with their own hearts because they are just not capable, and that their own human love is just not enough. I believe that God is love. Is it a God loving THROUGH me? I guess it could be! But if that's true, it's because I'm allowing such a thing… because it's literally who I am."

'Cause you're a sky, 'cause you're a sky full of stars
I'm gonna give you my heart
'Cause you're a sky, 'cause you're a sky full of stars
'Cause you light up the path
I don't care, go on and tear me apart
I don't care if you do, ooh
'Cause in a sky, 'cause in a sky full of stars
I think I saw you
'Cause you're a sky, 'cause you're a sky full of stars…

   - Coldplay

Nine
HONESTY, THE FINAL FRONTIER

"Ooh death.
Whooooah death…
won't you spare me over
'til another year."
– Ralph Stanley

Honesty about death and dying

"I am not afraid of dying. Any time will do. Why should I be afraid of dying? There's no reason for it."

- Pink Floyd

Wayne, from Atlanta wrote this… "Is there even one single verse in the Old Testament that clearly confirms life after death? This was an issue of intense debate in Jesus's time, maybe the biggest dividing issue of all. The Pharisees said there was a life after death, and the Sadducees said there was not. Both groups followed the same scriptures, so if they could not figure it out, I feel confident that there is no clear answer in the Old Testament. When Jesus was asked directly, he sided with the Pharisees, but it was on very weak ground, I would say a completely unconvincing turn of phrase."

"For the living know that they will die, but the dead know nothing; they have no further reward, and even their name is forgotten." (Ecclesiastes 9:5)

> *"Daylight comes to those who live*
> *but those who die they never see the sun come*
> *shining through their window pane they pass away.*
> *Silly girl to be a fool, you didn't play the golden rule,*
> *'Cos once you're through with one world,*
> *There's another waiting there."*
> *- Jeff Lynne (Electric Light Orchestra)*

Interestingly, the first half of this secular song lyric dogmatically states the same as Ecc. 9:5, and yet in the very next sentence the song writer states that there is another world awaiting us. Is there a "world" beyond this world when we die? I honestly don't know. I think that would be amazing, especially if we were able to traverse the universe, but no one knows for sure. I'm guessing that the ancient Egyptians also based their belief in an afterlife on N.D.E.s (near death experiences) just like many people of today do. For ancient Romans, upon death one was sent either to the Fields of Elysium, if one was a warrior or other type of hero, or to the Plain of Asphodel. Ancients from northwestern Europe called it Valhalla. In ancient Egypt, Sekhet-Aaru, or the Egyptian Reed Fields where Osiris rules. For the ancient aboriginal peoples – "dream time," or "eternal dreaming."

And what about N.D.E.s?

(an excerpt from my first book)

> If we objectively study thousands of N.D.E. experiences we will discover that they vary at about the same rate as U.F.O. sighting testimonies. This doesn't mean that they are not very real personal

experiences, but that they are simply not scientific evidence of any solid, definitive conclusion, nor can they be used as a responsible or reliable source for supporting any doctrine.

Interestingly, there are not two N.D.E.s alike. And if someone actually made it to a place called "heaven," then they could start a club with other people who could then describe the exact same location, including landmarks and distinguishing features. They could say, "Oh, you too? You saw the two towers by the crystal river too?"... The reason there are not two of these (millions of) experiences alike is because much (if not all) of those few seconds is being (unknowingly) manufactured by each individual's brain (because of every thought during one's lifetime of overheard conversations, teachings, imaginings of death, the afterlife, heaven, hell, rejoining loved ones, hopes, fears, desires, doctrines, beliefs), etc...

Some, in that state of higher consciousness, are even able to access secret information about the family (of which they are intimately/socially connected to) of which they "couldn't have known"... Some evangelical churches like to showcase any dark and scary NDE they can get their hands on to use as "support" for their doctrine on "hell"... But an extremely small, almost insignificant number of people have dark and scary NDE experiences. The vast majority of the millions of NDE's (regardless of religious or cultural background) are positive and peaceful.

Some fly over valleys and lush, green meadows like an eagle, some see flames, torment, and screaming, some see Grandpa and the family dog, some see streets of gold and an actual throne (that surprisingly looks a lot like a Medieval Times early English throne), some see a river and a field of onion plants, one man saw "the rapture" and heard a voice saying "Tell them! Tell them!", and, believe it or not, some even see that really hot blonde chick they always wished they'd asked out back in high school, sitting on a brand new Harley

Davidson - with the old Abba song "Knowing me, knowing you" playing on the bike's speakers...

Final point being made... None of the "testimonies" beyond that initial two or three seconds can be used in any way to build doctrine or even to establish something specific about a certain religion. But they are very entertaining. They tell us more about the person than what awaits the rest of us beyond death's door, if anything at all.

An excerpt from Field of Grasshoppers

Why Do We Have to Die? A dear Christian woman recently asked me this question: "Why do we have to die?" Please stop for a minute and really think about that question. My answer was simple: Everyone has to die. It is a part of nature, and always has been. Our body will die for the same reason a raccoon or a deer eventually dies. The reason it bothers us is because some well-meaning religious men have told us that there is possibly some way around it. There is not. The taught belief that there is has been a huge disservice to mankind, in my opinion - for theologians to wrongfully teach that some of us may not have to endure that natural transition! They have (literally) convinced people that death of the body is somehow because of some 'original sin' that an ancient human committed that affected the rest of humanity for all time. This is not true, and never has been true. Between that belief and the hell doctrine, the psychological damage has been done, which causes innocent people to fear the dying process, and be obsessed with thoughts of an afterlife that is either comforting or terrifying. Our bodies eventually dying are as much a part of nature as the leaves turning red, orange, and brown in the fall. Again, it actually is the truth that sets us free, not hopeful alternatives to the truth.

No escape from physical death is not a sad, meaningless, or purposeless story. It is actually an amazingly-beautiful story called "nature." The fact that nature has been demonized by religion as something that comforting alternatives are needed for is another subject altogether. But there is not nature and then also SUPERnature. There is nature that we understand scientifically, and then there is nature that we do not yet fully understand scientifically.

Bottom line? LIFE is absolutely incredible, regardless of anything, including death.

Whether or not there is life after death matters not. However, the fully-enjoyed, fully-embraced awesomeness of the here-and-now in this natural world is not only downplayed in religious circles, but actually painted as a place we should all be glad to one day be leaving...

We have all heard those songs...

"And I don't feel at home in this world anymore..." Or, as one contemporary Christian song says, "This world is not my home. Take this world and give me Jesus. This is not where I belong..."

What do we know about dying?

What do we actually know about dying – compared to what we believe about dying?

One of my most valued friends says that we are eternal beings who have always lived... like the old C. S. Lewis quote... "You don't have a soul. You are a soul. You have a body." And I believed this for most of my life, but I am now starting to question that whole way of thinking. Part of me would like that very much, but the logical side of me says, "Please provide even a little evidence."

While in a conversation with a guy who was claiming that my more naturalist philosophy was dogmatic, he said this... "Ken, YOU don't die, your BODY dies. But that body is not YOU." When I asked him if he has any evidence of this belief, he replied... "I would like to give you some proof, but this 'knowing' comes from within me, and would be classified as intuitive, rather than empirical." I do appreciate his sincerity, I really do, but there are millions of people who also "empirically know" that Jesus is coming back here someday, riding on a horse in actual clouds.

> *"We all have two lives.*
> *The second one starts*
> *when we realize*
> *we only have one."*
>
> *- Tom Hiddleston*

My friend Jim High shared this… "To suppose any existence after we die, is to suppose that we began at birth on this Earth, but will then for some strange reason life changes and we live forever. Or maybe we lived somewhere else before we were born, but we don't remember it. So most probably we didn't. Why would we think we exist after we die? And will we know who we use to be? If not, it matters not. Better to understanding that life evolved on planet Earth and through 3.5 billion years of evolution has resulted in us. We are evolved from the great apes, the caveman and the cabbages, too. Do we think they all went to some other life when they died? Seems to me from what I know about LIFE, this one life I am living is it. When I die it will be over and I'll be no more. How can nothing be scary? You wouldn't even know you are dead. Think about a sound night of sleep without any dreams. If you never woke up you would not know you never woke up. You would not know you died in your sleep. And when your image and idea of a God gets corrected from those false images that Christianity holds on to - you will understand even better that this is your one-time shot at being human. This ought to make us want to be the best humans we can be, and leave our world better than we found it."

"Gravity… wants to bring me down"

Gravity, rust, aging, and yes, death itself are not the results of some ancient curse, but as much a part of nature as the turning of the leaves in autumn. Ancient men making stuff up because they didn't like the harsher realities of nature, or wishing it was something other than what it vividly shows itself to be, is something humankind has been doing for thousands of years. But reality IS enough. Yes, it is. It should be more appreciated and accepted for what it is, not more redefined and romanced into something weird and spooky to relieve our discomfort with creative scenarios of religious fantasy. The simple, obvious truth has never been as popular as the romanticized, poeticized, spiritualized, religionized "truth." But most people are not looking for simple, obvious truth. They are hungry for *comforting* truth. And this ... taught need for comfort, and comforting alternatives for nature, is often more desired than truth itself.

In defense of a God and an afterlife, a preacher named Bertie told me, "Ken, you may have grown up in a pleasant environment with loving and caring parents, and so it may be easy for you to not see the value in the comfort the grace message offers. But what about all the people and children who are being abused? There are many people in the world who are suffering greatly. They need that hope..."

My answer to Bertie is this... When someone is trying to sell a used car, they usually romance the positive things about the vehicle, but more often than not don't make it that much of a priority to give the short list of what doesn't always work on the car. Likewise, when we tell people that a God loves and cares for them more than their own family does, we may want to also tell them to disregard all the vivid, life evidence of just the opposite. And one of my friends recently said, "You lose no credibility when selling heaven to people, because dead people never ask for their money back."

Kevin Sturges, from Milwaukee writes, "Nobody really knows what happens after we die. There are reasonable ideas on any number of possibilities. At least, at the very worst, when we die... nothing at all happens... and our bodies are recycled back into nature where we came from. That might sound incredibly sad at first, especially when we think of our loved humans and animals, but if you get used to the idea, there's also a certain poetically deep beauty to it that is actually meaningful... Just peace... eternal sleep... No more sadness, or loneliness, or crying for the suffering of your loved ones. Just peace and rocking in the arms of the eternally transcending Universe... All we really know is that we have NOW.

So make the best of your short time here. Treat others well. Enjoy, and taste all good things fully. Don't waste a minute letting other people make you afraid to fully discover and be yourself. How could anyone go wrong or be judged for doing that?"

Honesty about evidence of a God

To many theists, someone claiming there is no God-Person, invisible or not, seems utterly ridiculous. And yet it never once dawns on them that the BULK of the actual evidence leans more heavily in the naturalist model. In these last few pages of the book I would like the reader to draw out their own inner honesty, and begin to ask the question... What operational dynamic best harmonizes with nature and observable reality... a (hiding) King-like anthropomorphic invisible Entity/Guy with very human-like characteristics, or a more nature-based law of attraction model that is perfectly and consistently impersonal and wondrously indifferent? And the second question... Which of these models needs to be romanced indefinitely in order to preserve its viability? We can give the name "God" to whatever Energy Source operates and sustains the universe, but what we cannot do is make that Source love and care about us more than our family and friends do.

Honesty about new religions

I'm not a big fan of joining a new religion to replace the one I left... I've already done that several times to get where I currently am both theologically and philosophically...

Being that the last couple of years of my journey traveled through the path of Buddhist and Taoist writings as well as several others that would be considered by some as "new-age" philosophies, a dear concerned friend told me, "Ken, so many people nowadays are leaving traditional religion and becoming so fascinated with all things 'Eastern.' Eastern cures, Eastern herbs and incense, Eastern philosophy and religion. Why is that? Is it just the idea of something new and different?

But "traditional religion" means one thing in the West and another thing in the East. Right? The East has actually been around a few hundred thousand years more than the west, so perhaps "traditional" more accurately describes the philosophies of the EAST, and not as "newer" than our adopted religion, but actually, and quite literally - older.

Replacing cigarettes with obesity because of ice cream and cheese can produce the same lethal results. And replacing one religion with yet another religion is still a (taught) obsession for permission to finally view oneself as significant. As long as we are searching, digging, and studying to hopefully establish our significance, we are still very much "in religion," whether that religion be evangelical fundamentalism or one of the many new-age philosophies of our time. The truth is… we are as significant as we will ever be, and we have never needed a license for it.

Recently a person named Shawn reminded me that even though we leave one religion, thinking that we are "free from religion," it is often just another one to replace the one we left. Shawn says, "Same church, different pew."

There's actually a great deal of validity to this statement… we go from one religion to the next to the next to the next, and then on to the next. This, however, is a positive, productive, and progressive thing for many people – a journey of discovery that must take place. Even making a radical jump from theism directly into atheism can be categorized as "a new religion to replace the last one." I really don't like all the "isms" and "ists" but if I am to be honest with myself - I probably fall into one of those categories myself… probably leaning more toward the natural (ist) camp. I spent a considerable amount of time and devotion in the new-age and new-thought camps, and yes… I was still searching for significance and purpose and meaning…still hoping to find some … mystical "reasons" for why things work as they do. Looking back now I recognize that I was still very much in that religious mindset.

I sincerely feel that the closer we get to a progressively-more-objective attempt at being honest about nature and the naturalist model - the closer we do get to moving away from the more religious, mystical mindsets. None of us are "perfectly objective," and there's really no reason for competition between ourselves on this subject. I look at the entire life process as a never ending education into an explorative, inquisitive wonder and awe... much like a child exploring and trying to figure out certain parts of nature. And isn't that what we are all really doing? And is there really some sort of ... eternal danger of getting it all wrong if we don't study with the right group of people? Probably not.

"What you ought to do..."

There is no "what you should be doing" or "what you're supposed to be doing"... An insecure salesman sold us that - so he would not be so alone in his insecurities. Follow your heart, not other people's "shoulds" or "supposed to's". We make what we consider to be healthy choices for ourselves that give us inner peace and more vibrancy of life, if that's what we want, that is... and that's enough. And yes, it really is enough.

Honesty about cars, planes, and Isaac Stern

Too Beautiful to Comprehend... Perhaps the reason we find it so difficult to even imagine there being millions of billions of other worlds out there with intelligent life, is because of our own beauty. We look at the things we have built - everything from forming a coffee cup out of clay, to the magnificent intricacies of a jet airliner - and it is so amazing to us that our minds simply cannot comprehend other completely unrelated worlds to have been able to evolve to the point of accomplishing the same or more. And yet, if we were to actually stop and consider the sheer size and scope of the known universe, the mathematical probabilities in and of themselves yield nothing short of an almost certainty of our planet's beauties of life being duplicated and multiplied millions of billions of times throughout the cosmos. If not, the known universe would sure seem like a lot of wasted, meaningless space. Would it not?

Do this... take the time to sit on a hill overlooking any major city, with its steel and glass sky scrapers and precision-paved freeways. Then travel back just 300 years and you'll only see a half dozen people on horses slowly making their way down a winding dirt trail. Think about this for a minute... In less than three lifetimes the human species has figured out how to fly, how to cut steel with water, and have basically built everything your eyes see when looking at your city. This industrialized high-tech world we now live in is all about human ingenuity and the technological advancement of our species. Just because it is amazing to us does not mean that there must be a Master Designer out there somewhere with the characteristics of a human.

Honesty about the unverifiable past and future

(excerpt from What Is God, And How Does It Work?)

Bigger-Than-Life, Reality-Defying Miracles... The trouble is... where did they go? I'm not talking about physical healing or a prayer being answered. I'm talking about events like the Noah's ark story, or the Red Sea story, the Sampson story, huge city walls crumbling to the earth because of people blowing hand-made trumpets, God literally stopping the spin of our planet for a few hours so the Israelites could kill more enemy soldiers, burning bushes, talking snakes, pillars of fire in the sky, God talking in a loud voice to someone, etc. Why is it that all these kinds of bigger-than-life, reality-defying miracles either took place in the way-far-off distant, unverifiable past or are supposedly yet to occur sometime in the way-far-off distant, unverifiable future? And all the time in between these two time periods.... um... well... the sound of cars on the freeway, a neighbor's dog barking, and a vapor trail left in the sky by an airliner. Hmmm... Be honest... have you ever stood on your back deck, listening to the evening crickets and really stopped to think about this? Is it even a possibility that many of these Bible stories were actually "stories" rather than actual, literal events? And such events ... stopped happening at one point in history... because... why?

When was the last time anyone saw a guy in his Honda Accord floating up into the stratosphere because he was spiritually close enough to God to skip the dying process, like the guy in the chariot in the Old Testament? And the children in Ethiopia could really use a manna-from-heaven event right now in the 21st-century. Nope. Nada. Just the sound of the hot, desert wind and a baby crying from hunger pains. Is it even possible, that right now what is outside your back door, is what has always been and will always be (other than the improvements mankind will make over the next millennia)? The truth has never been hidden from us. It is actually the most vivid thing there is. Is it possible that since we do not like that, we have chosen to believe in ancient, comforting mythology over reality? Have we seriously lost the ability to use our logic and deductive reasoning on things like this?

Honesty about nature, and SUPERnature...

(excerpt from What Is God, And How Does It Work?)

The main trouble with nature is that it is more (or in some cases less) than we want it to be. If we were to get to the bottom of our feelings about nature, we would find that we don't want it to be as beautiful or tragic as it actually is. There's not "nature" and then "super-nature", especially if nature is God's creation. Imagine God saying, "Hey... If you liked my nature, then you're really going to like my SUPER-nature!" Doesn't that sound silly? Of course it does, but many have been convinced of this very contradictive thing. Mankind wasn't satisfied with nature, so they called anything they couldn't understand in nature - God's SUPER-nature, adding a few extras of their own.

Without argument, nature is the most consistent, never-changing, always-faithful, ever-present, no-respecter-of-persons, same-yesterday-today-and-forever, out-in-the-light-to-be-seen-for-exactly-what-it-is thing in the universe, and that may be precisely why man has come up with all sorts of psychologically-comforting alternatives for it. If man is afraid of anything, it is not "the devil," or even the future, but nature and reality. The fact that nature is incapable of changing is probably the most frightening thing of all. We can deal with the mysteries and the hidden stuff, and all the religious mythology, because we can make things up about it and define it all in any number of ways we choose to help us sleep at night. It is the all-too-obvious facts of life/reality that we dislike, partly because we know we look like fools when we try explaining them away.

The dying process is just one example of this... In reality, there is probably not an actual location somewhere outside of earth's atmosphere where any of us "go" when our bodies die here. This magnificent atmosphere-protected ecological paradise we call Earth is traveling through empty space at a speed of 67 THOUSAND miles per hour! Why would it make any logical sense for one particular life form here to leave this amazing life-sustaining system when they die? It wouldn't. There are 100 billion solar systems just within our own galaxy, and 500 billion other galaxies out there. Why would we need to leave this one? Why would that even make sense? These utopian beliefs are mythological in nature, and constructed only for our comfort – that there is some "better world" awaiting us out there somewhere in the great by-and-by. Will I see my dad again someday? I would sure like that. I would like that very much. The truth is - no one knows.

What if all of life's answers have always been right out in front of us, and just as clear and simple as the turning of autumn leaves? Is that even possible?

The biggest "trouble" with nature is that it never lies or contradicts itself.

Honesty about what is, and what is not

We become 100 percent responsible for our own lives, our own demeanor, our own personal growth and development, our own happiness and our own mental health the day we finally dismiss our invisible imaginary friends and foes, and not a moment before. There is not only great freedom in this, but a newly-revealed empowerment and exciting potential for life and living. I often wondered if such freedom were even possible, but at the same time always somehow knew it was mine all along. Perhaps I just didn't have the understanding to claim it.

The truth? We already created much of how we will experience today, and we did it yesterday, the day before that, or maybe a few days ago, or months ago — when our choices, thoughts, desires, intentions and reactions brought into motion much of the world that is unfolding out in front of us. We all acknowledge there are some things that are beyond our control, but there are more things in our control and responsibility than we were led to believe.

Although this is a book about honesty, please understand that this is a story about my honesty, not yours. Each person must process everything they hear in their own way, and according to their own feelings about what they have read, what has been said, and how they feel about it all.

Some of the questions I had to ask myself

Is there really some eternal, cosmic hero person named Jesus whose invisible spirit lives inside of people? Is such an entity really "my friend"? When we say, "I love

HONESTY, THE FINAL FRONTIER

Jesus," do we actually mean we "love" what we were told we are supposed to love? Do we really "know" a man from the first century? Or do we know what we've been *told* about him? I've met Christians who said they "knew" Jesus thirty years ago as a Judge who would one day be telling millions of people "Depart from Me, I never knew you," but since then have completely changed their position on eternal damnation. But wait a minute... did they really "know" Jesus then if they thought that was who he was, but now no longer do? Wouldn't that mean that what they actually knew was what they had been *told* about him? Do they attribute the good results and great, unexplainable things in life as actual acts of this Jesus person because that is how their positive experiences have been defined and translated for them? Did this first-century person really physically float up into the stratosphere to then reside somewhere in outer space? Is there really some ... hierarchy/Boss mechanism/judicial-based Ruler/King of the universe who made some intergalactic rules of how or where we spend eternity? Is our belief in one particular Christian doctrine the only one way to achieve eligibility for that eternal realm called heaven when we die? Did Jesus really get tempted by an actual "devil" in the wilderness? If he was all alone out there in the desert, who recorded it in the words we have read about that account? Does most of our "Higher Power" comfort actually come from our own thinking and working things out in our own minds?

Do I really end up in court when I die because of what I did or did not do, or did or did not believe during my short 90 years in Arizona? Is there really a "Him" or a "He," or is it all more of a quite nature-based system or ... organic energy/source matrix-like program that we are all interacting with (or as)? Do we really know? Is there really some sort of ... magical "power" in the blood of some first-century spiritual leader? Does one's mental devotion to a God actually buy us some sort of favor, or ... trigger some sort of mystical impartation of "heavenly" inspiration, provision, or eternal life? If we offer up our very hearts in a devoted mental style, in absolute belief, to a God-Person Entity out there somewhere, is there really such a cosmic, invisible Entity who then rewards us for such doctrine-based allegiance?

Have you ever heard your inherited faith described with the wording I just used? Is this not in essence what many of us have been taught? Do we really have a "God-shaped hole" in our lives that only a God can fill and satisfy? This is something every battered wife certainly understands... Imagine for a minute what you would think of me if I told my wife she has a big Ken-sized hole in her life that only I could ever fill. Some of my religious mentors gave this a more positive spin by saying, "God just wants what's best for us – because He loves us so much." But why is it that every time I heard that I imagined a man in a sleeveless t-shirt standing over a woman with a subservient look on her face? In my world, any true "love" that requires or expects something in return for that "love" is not love at all, but mafia-like tyranny. And sure, theologians for decades have been selling this as "walking in covenant with God," but boil that all the way down and what you (really) have is a quite conditional-love God who basically makes deals with humans... trading provisions for worship.

Have I "fallen from Grace"? Or have I "risen to reason"? Does anyone really believe that some sort of century-long conversion contest between the world's two largest religions is what will eventually achieve world peace and unity? Does anyone actually believe that? Is it really true that everyone who departs from their parent's faith is either angry or hurt or bitter or had some hurtful experience with a local church? Isn't it even possible that some really have outgrown some of the beliefs of their predecessors? No?

"Hey! Teacher! Leave them kids alone!"

Many people are still convinced that we need a "He." But is this not a growth-stunting thing? Is this not all about personal insecurity of not being enough without a "Him"? But think about this... I mean really think about it... Without a "Him," would we really not be enough? Would our lives really fall apart at the seams? Would the sunsets and sunrises really lack beauty? Would the birth of a newborn child be less amazing? I think not. Have we been trained to think that perhaps paying some invisible Entity compliments will result in a higher level of personal significance? Really? Are we not already as significant as we can be all on our own? Are we not already enough? Haven't we always been enough?

A Christian friend of mine said, "Yes, Ken, we are enough IF we sprung from the earth all on our own, and acquired self-awareness all by our own power. But we are NOT the source of our own being."

I do understand where my friend is coming from, but why would we be "not enough" if we evolved? Are the deer and the eagle "not enough"? My friend's line of thinking would simply mean that if we were created premeditatedly – we somehow OWE that Creator some sort of … payment, even if that payment is a continual stream of adoration-filled compliments. It is a very real possibility that there is no "He" or a "She" or a "Them" or some cosmic, invisible "Person" or personality with all of our human-like characteristics the Christian Bible defines nature to be.

The words "Whatever brought about the universe" is NOT an acceptable sentence to most Theists. To them, such a phrase wreaks of irreverence, pride, and a lack of gratitude for having been created. In their minds, even a bowl of corn flakes should be acknowledged as an undeserved gift "from the Father above." Am I not being honest here about the evangelical culture many of us grew up in? Ask yourself why… I mean really ask yourself - why it is so important for some that nature be looked at as an invisible, Santa-like "Guy"? It is important to them because they have been convinced that this whole "owing" thing is actually not an owing thing at all, but rather a sweet, even natural response to the great benevolence of a loving Creator – Who is allowing them to be alive, breathe the air, and eat corn flakes. If they were honest they would all reject any such similar relationship with their spouse, but have unknowingly, and warmly adopted just such a "marriage" with a quite legal-based, demanding heavenly Husband – who wants to be worshipped.

Am I being too harsh here, or am I being too honest? At the very roots of this entire thing is a taught insecurity… of which the only solution offered is a God that requires acknowledgment, respect, and devotion. But has this ever been the (actual) case in reality?

This all reminds me very much of the unspoken, unwritten message of religion… "You need me. Without me you are just not enough."

Honesty about "Belonging before you believe"?

("The body" or "comradery" or simply finding "You"?)

That whole ... "be like us, it's beautiful"... using-arrogance-to-sell-humility thing left a really bad taste in my mouth...

In my town there are a couple of small groups of church folks who have rented out places like the junior high school auditorium on Sunday mornings to hold their meetings. Most of these small groups are the result of break-aways from some other church that just wasn't teaching the "full" gospel, or the "correct" gospel. On a small wooden fold-out sign they placed on the main street were the words, "Belong Before You Believe." I recently read an article on a church website about youth department growth and retention, where I found this statement... "Today's youth want to belong before they believe. So if you hope to get them to embrace our church doctrines, embrace them first." But what does this mean? This almost sounds like "sales" training to me. Is that like... "Hey dude. Cool skateboard! Wanna come to my church and hang out with some REALLY cool skater dudes?" Am I the only one who sees the ... unrealness here?

And the whole ... "belong before you believe" thing would probably work – just as long as you can eventually be swayed into believing the same as they do. Because if you suddenly came to some rather different theological conclusions, and started sharing them with the group, they would be the first ones to tell you that you "probably don't 'belong' here anymore."

I remember when I was a church-attending man hearing the frequently-used term "the body," or ... "the body of Christ." The term "Christ" of course, in those circles, meant a truly magical, cosmic Person, in fact an all-powerful "God Himself" as a human – in much of the same way some sort of electrical power base runs and governs all the many functioning parts of a well-oiled machine. And, as the doctrine goes... none of the functioning parts of the machine can do anything without the electric motor Power Source. In fact, they are (basically) worthless without the electricity... you know... like a branch that is no longer "connected" to a tree. In this case - Jesus being the tree, and faith-based declarations and heart-felt devotion and worship somehow ... firmly connecting you to that Jesus-Power Source (much like the very magical/DNA connection we saw in the movie Avatar between the flying dragons and their riders). Hence the continual exhortation to be "planted" in "the house of the Lord"... It was thought of in the same way the "bond" between flying dragon and rider was so very important.

But what is this whole ... "belonging" business about? We've all heard it said that people want to "belong" to something... be a part of something... you know... "the body", etc...

Are we not talking here about comradery?

You know... a bunch of people getting together with similar interests and beliefs? Recently I attended an amazing rock concert at the Key Arena in Seattle. The kinship and oneness was so thick there... people singing along, some waiving their hands, some actually in tears because the music struck such a deep chord within them of some powerful sense of, well... belonging. I have a coworker who is an avid rider of horses, and is passionately involved in a Medieval Times professional jousting club. He finds and experiences great comradery and kinship there, developing meaningful, lasting, lifetime friendships with those he interacts with. I know of a young girl who is a major participant in adoption programs for greyhounds nationwide. And the social benefits of her involvement with that group of enthusiasts goes much deeper than just finding homes for dogs. There are hundreds of reasons different people come together to share and be enriched with what they all have in common. Have you ever been to a major air show, or hot air balloon lift, or the Washington State Annual Kite Festival?

Some groups get together for entertainment, some for charitable causes, some for a passionate interest or recreation they all share, some for philosophical reasons, some for rehabilitation from alcoholism, and some folks come together for reasons of comfort – wherein they give each other affirmations of how "everything is going to be alright just as long as you believe the correct things about yourself and God... and just as long as you remain a part of this particular 'body' of believers... and since pastors Bob and Linda are so wonderful at teaching us all the things we need to be perpetually mindful of, we need to support them financially (so they can continue teaching us all the things we need to be perpetually mindful of)." There's nothing wrong with that if that is your choice, or need for comradery, but let's please be honest here about what things really are and what they are not.

It's okay if you need that sort of thing in order to get through the week. Like millions of others, I just no longer do. Singing actual does work just fine for me, like James Taylor sang. Plus, I would much rather hang out with some really cool island folks who love to surf and cook seafood on the beach. They are so friendly, so accepting and real!

Once I understood that all seven billion humans in this world ARE a "part of one body" (whether they know it yet or not) and also already ARE very connected branches to one tree (whether they know it yet or not), my search for significance was over. Something else that was also very over was "trying" to love my neighbor "as myself." I no longer needed to force myself into sales philosophy gimmicks or taught benevolent-mindsets in order to embrace people. You know... with the secret, unspoken strategy to ultimately "win them" into my particular belief system... which was supposedly the only place they could experience the "real" love and the "real" joy and the "real" peace. So I thought...

Love your neighbor AS yourself

The truth about loving my neighbor AS myself was finally and completely understood. There is a REASON some religious folks have to ask a God to "love people through them," basically asking God to do their neighbor-loving FOR them. And the reason for this is because they (actually) recognize that their own humanitarian love is simply not as sincere as their hearts know it should be. Why? Because they are being told to do something that their own doctrines cannot allow them to do... judge their neighbors as "them" and love them as "themselves" at the same time. Impossible.

I remember asking God to "Please show me the hurting, and oh Lord let me see them through YOUR eyes!" And yet now, looking back, I realize that I already saw the hurting ones and I already cared about them. There was nothing wrong with my heart, but there was something horribly wrong with a philosophy that literally kept me from being able to honestly love from a sincere, truly non-judgmental place. What I didn't understand was that until I truly SAW others AS myself (as already members of the same body as fellow earthlings, with no separation) I COULDN'T "love them as myself" because they WEREN'T "myself," they were "them" and we were "us." And they would always be "them" as long as they believed differently than me. It is so good to be free to love and care from an honest, sincere, truly free, genuine heart.

> *"We must learn to be aware of our position in life.*
> *Deeply know that there is nothing that can drive your*
> *world other than what you give the reigns to...*
> *so take them back."*
> *- Jim High*

Honesty about the reality of being enough

You are beautiful because you are, period. Until I realized that I was enough, my own humanitarian love was enough, my heart was enough, I was good enough, I was innocent enough, I was beautiful enough, I was significant enough - I spent most of my life, one brick at a time, building a wall around my heart in some sad, unworthy, not-enoughness, unhealthy self-esteem-maintenance program that quite literally hid my own light ("under a bushel," as they say in that old children's Sunday school song).

The teaching that says, "You are beautiful but you're not beautiful, but you are, but you're not" is beyond confusing, not to mention self-imprisoning. It is so good to be free from such insanity!

Gold, Frankincense, and Myrrh...

Guilt, fear, and low self-esteem are actually warmly-held, devotion-based treasures to some folks - as they have been taught to see them as a fitting gift of myrrh, frankincense, and gold for their God.

When my father died I grieved so badly that it turned into physical illness for me. When someone suggested I get professional help or medication, I blurted out in deep, emotional, turmoil... "My father deserves my grief!!!"

My wife quickly responded with... "Ken! My goodness! Your father would expect no such thing from you!" Then she held me in her arms as I was reduced to tears of healing.

If you think by losing your treasured fear you would then also lose your reverence, you're just flat out wrong.

In short, we were all born completely innocent, completely significant, more than completely enough, with absolutely no need for some sort of legal absolution for being born a human rather than a deer, and then we were taught otherwise by people we trusted. This is one of the saddest truths we will ever come to grips with. Many people will not discover this until they are in the latest days of the winter of their lives. Very close to "criminal" in my opinion...

Question:
If you take away all my adopted campfire legends,
ancient folklore, inherited mysticism, and
Santa-like fairytales, then what hope do I have left?

Answer:
Who told you that reality isn't enough?
That's the person we should really be
questioning and investigating.

It's not a puzzle.
It's a planet.

This may actually be
the whole lesson.

Ten

CUT THE CORD! (CUT!)

By the cold and religious we were taken in hand
Shown how to feel good and told to feel bad.
Tongue tied and terrified we learned how to pray
Now our feelings run deep and cold as the clay.
  - Roger Waters

You know what?
I'm done here.
No, I mean it. I really am...
Done, that is.

This small chapter was actually inspired by a musical masterpiece from a heavy metal band called "Shinedown." In an interview the singer said that anything in your life that is holding you back from a full life is not a good thing, and that you should cut it lose... cut that cord.

I'm not in the habit of cutting my relationships with people who believe differently than me, mainly because I've had a few people who cut me out of their conversations or any interactions of philosophical honesty when they learned I no longer believed the same as them. That was all the inspiration I needed for what *not* to do to people who are different than me. I am no longer afraid to entertain other life-philosophies that differ sharply from the ones I inherited. Why should I be? Once you get to the point where any and all conversations are not only welcome, but encouraged, you have lost an element of social fear that many are still constrained by. I've talked at length about this unfortunate reality in a couple of other books. What we are discussing here is getting to the point of finally recognizing unhealthy life philosophies and self-views that cannot result in consistent, sustainable personal growth.

There comes a time, and that time has definitely come for me, when one severs the cord that has anchored them to ideologies that keep them from moving onward to new levels of life, freedom, wellness, and abundance. The whole "getting ready, to get ready, to get ready" approach, although often a necessary part of one's journey, doesn't really ever free you until you come to that crossroad with the sign that says, "If all these things are not true, then you don't have to believe (or fear) them anymore."

There's always that Tuesday afternoon when we wake up and finally realize that it is okay, and it is not irreverent, and it is not eternally dangerous to seriously question mythology-like stories of talking snakes, ancient curses, and golden cities in outer space. And this is a very liberating thing for so many. "You may say I'm a dreamer, ..."

"Goodnight Auberge, I leave you now..."

For me personally, it was a matter of surrendering to observable reality and finally accepting the full responsibility for my own life, my own love, my own integrity, and my own life's potentials. This very book IS that turning point for me, that final cord-cutting ceremony, if you will. And although I am VERY excited about my next two books that are already well underway, there will be no more books from me showcasing the stark differences between religion and reality. These first five books have been extremely important for me to write, as they have also made a huge impact on so many people around our world. At first this was a major shock for me to learn that I was not at all alone in my experiences. I receive letters and emails on a weekly basis from people asking me to never stop writing on all the subjects I have covered in my books. But that's just it – I *have* fully covered virtually everything I possibly could on this part of my journey.

Without even knowing it, by simply telling my personal story I ended up being the mouthpiece for thousands of others who were also wondering if they were alone. I simply put into thoughtful wording what others were already experiencing. So … I certainly do not see myself as some sort of philosophical guru with new, breakthrough information that no one else has thought of before. This book is merely a mirrored reflection of a million stories just like mine. These first few books have been a very important part of many people's journeys, but still just a *part*, like one of many chapters of our lives. But there comes a time for moving on to the next chapter of our growth process. I am presently working on a novel as well as a book of poetic inspiration and encouragement.

> *"Oh… this old world keeps spinning round*
> *It's a wonder tall trees ain't layin down*
> *There comes a time…"*
> *- Neil Young*

I am humbled and so very honored from all the support and feedback and accolades for my work thus far, and I hope my next offering will deliver even more inspiration, and a deeper connection with my readers than all five of my first books did. That is my goal.

"Hey you, out there beyond the wall…"

> *"There is nothing to find,*
> *there is nowhere to go,*
> *there is nothing to achieve or attain.*
> *Eventually, you discover this,*
> *and you are free."*
>
> *- Jim Palmer*

My friend, Danny Randall says this, "I'm loving my journey out of religion and into real life. In order for me to be free I had to let go of attempting to process things through a religious grid altogether. It meant seeing and viewing my life as it is without enforcing a religious paradigm to somehow make it 'fit' in my head and be able to understand and quantify it all. It means my life is beautiful, glorious, messy, and incredibly enough on its own. I don't have to figure out who or what 'God' is or how He/She/It fits into my experiences anymore.

I am no longer preoccupied with needing answers to an afterlife, a heaven, a hell, whether or not Jesus is God, or what the 'right' answers are to anything. Now it's enough to follow my heart. It's enough to be true to myself. I don't have to convert anyone over to my way of thinking and I don't have to fear the validity of other's views that may contradict or challenge my own.

I am free to let my own soul be my teacher. I am free to allow myself to learn from anyone and anything I experience in life. And most of all I am free to enjoy life without constantly needing an agenda or some 'greater purpose' having to drive me.

If you are wrestling with deconstructing or attempting to reconstruct your faith, here is my advice to you: walk away from it all. Stop trying to understand. Stop attempting to build a new or improved belief system. Just live. Laugh and enjoy the company of your kids, spouse, family and friends! Go for a swim or a hike. Read a good book that has nothing to do with spirituality. Watch your favorite television show. It's all sacred and it's all beautiful. Be present to what's right in front of you and allow yourself to let go of the search. You are already significant."

The ocean sunset and the incoming waves are not beautiful. What is beautiful is how your eyes see it all. And so, the "beauty of the ocean," believe it or not, is (actually) YOU.

Eleven
THE AUTHOR'S CONTENTION…

My contention throughout all of this work is that life is not complicated, and it never was. Life is NOT the result of ancient curses, magical cosmic heroes, or correctly-translated antique religious writings from some small regional Mediterranean tribe. The idea that one of the main reasons we are here is to get safely to somewhere else via properly-believed procedure and protocol is just not true, and it never was true. Nor are several other of the mythology-like narratives we have been taught accurate to reality. There are things our hearts instinctively know that our indoctrinated heads are still calling the shots on. There are times and events in our lives that get us closer to accepting this "knowing" of our hearts. This brutal, raw honesty about what observable reality out here in the real world vividly shows us (compared to what we've been *taught* it shows us) is the turning point for many in our generation. And no longer believing in a Santa-Claus-like invisible Being is NOT a thing to be feared or in any way worried about. Most of these things we have believed were because we were *told* to believe them at a very young age. They are "facts" in our minds, not because such things have any actual proof, but because all of our experiences have been explained *FOR* us as interactions and results of those mythological narratives.

HONESTY: THE FINAL FRONTIER

These unprotected moments, or ... glimpses of honesty and intuition bring us right up next to the vivid, naked truth about ourselves, the world we live in, and how things truly work here. And yet even in these most optimum settings in which we could make that jump from our indoctrinated heads to our hearts - we often still don't quite grasp those seemingly just-out-of-reach simplicities of life. "There must be something more!" we shout, as we cling to our inherited beliefs. Much easier it is, and often more ... comforting (or comfortable) to just ... "decide" that the old information *is* all the information. It isn't, and our hearts have always known it.

Most of my life was like being in a never-ending high school chemistry class, but it wasn't worms or frogs we were trying to dissect, but the air itself, completely convinced by our mentors that we could really be that 1 out of 40,000 other denominations who finally "got it right." And we sincerely believed we somehow owed our God such an impassioned search for the meaning of everything. We thought to ourselves... "After all, what better compliment to a God than spending your entire life trying to figure Him out?"

PS: Scientists have already figured out the air, and exactly how it works.

I'm now 60 years old as I close this book, but I didn't truly start living my own life until about five years ago. Before that I was perpetually obsessed with the lives and times of people from some other ancient culture... hanging on their every word as some sort of eternally-consequential coded message from a God for some ... *proper way* I was supposed to be living, thinking, and seeing the world and myself from ... all the while thinking that this was "living." It wasn't. And like I said, it was like trying to dissect the air. I wasn't living from my own heart at all as a truly free man, but from someone else's religion-based anthropomorphic translations and explanations for nature.

But here's what I'm going to do about it... Everything I CAN so that at least 10,000 other people don't make the same mistake. Life is too short not to be who you truly are, and not to love who you truly are.

We are warned not to listen to the progressive voices of our generation, and so we don't seriously investigate or study what we really don't want to know. And we don't like to admit that about ourselves... Hence comfort becomes more

THE AUTHOR'S CONTENTION...

important to us than truth or reality itself. But brutal honestly and boldly facing the truth about the simplicities of nature and reality always does three main things...

1. Creates more freedom.
2. Kills more fear.
3. Empowers us with more personal responsibility.

All this time – the "truth that will set us free," is actually... truth itself, and simply having the courage and honesty of accepting whatever that is.

Honesty truly is...
... the Final Frontier

*Imagine…
at the end of your life
you finally realize
that you've always been free
and you've always been
enough.*

- Ken Dahl

The first four books in Ken's Shedding Religion series…

"If we would be a real seeker after truth, it is necessary that at least once in our lives we doubt, as far as possible, all things." - Rene Descartes (1596 - 1650)

Book #1. FIELD OF GRASSHOPPERS

Revised in March 2016: This book begins Ken's theological journey, starting at age six, growing up in an evangelical church background. It covers his theological evolution and progression through and finally out of his church's doctrines of eschatology (end times), the psychologically-damaging doctrine of hell, and the concept of God as a Judge of Whom everyone supposedly must face when they die. This book is a must read for open-minded Christians who have some serious questions about freedom and ultimately rediscovering the innocence they knew as a child.

Ken writes, "There is something natural about life, about the seasons of life, and even about God. As a child, my intuition told me that life's most significant mysteries can be solved without libraries full of books on theology. At a very young age, there was an obvious simplicity, an almost knowing, that all the hidden answers were going to somehow roll out in front of me like a soft, summer picnic blanket as I grew older. I don't know why or how I knew this: I just did.

Life Comes in Thirds… During our younger years, we are incessantly questioning everything the establishment throws our way. Then there are the middle years, when we have pretty much settled into most of it, even as odd as some of it seems. School, occupation, recreation, and our social life takes up our time and energy, leaving us with very little reason or desire to even question what we have long since accepted as truth. When we get older, we return to our childlike state, once again asking a never-ending list of questions. However, the difference then is that we are no longer asking how things are, but whether or not what we've been taught is correct or not. At this point, we have had the time to think about all the ideologies, philosophies, and doctrines, and see how they compare to the real world we've been living in. Some of it fits, some of it sort of fits, but we begin to realize that a bunch of it doesn't fit at all. Such was the case for me.

I'm returning to innocence. Don't try to stop me."

Book #2. WHAT IS GOD, AND HOW DOES IT WORK?

This is an extremely bold and brutally honest work, not only asking the really tough questions about the God of the Bible (compared to the sharply-conflicting picture real-life observable reality shows us), but it also does a responsible job showcasing the actual history of the God-concepts held by most theists. We favor comfort over truth. We have always been that way. It is what we were taught. It is what we know. It is no coincidence that most religious doctrines are comforting alternatives to some of the harsher realities of nature and the reality of normal, everyday life here.

For years we have been discussing what we don't know (as if we did), and what we do know (as if we didn't). This is a book for those who are not afraid to talk about what we do know, what we have seen, and what many others have been reluctant to talk about until now. It isn't information that we have lacked, but rather - brutal, fearless honesty. Perhaps what is really needed is not deeper studies into the doctrinal complexities of our current, inherited beliefs, but rather brave acceptance of the simplicity and naked truth of observable reality.

This book comes with a warning label – "You cannot unread what you have read here."

Book #3. REBUILDING THE VILLAGE

Author Jim Palmer writes, "Rebuilding the Village by Ken Dahl is an 'I have a dream' book. It is all those things – subversive, transformative, and liberative. In his first two books, Field Of Grasshoppers, and What Is God, And How Does It Work?, Ken questions, deconstructs and clears the decks of those false religious and cultural beliefs, mindsets, narratives and ideologies that have kept humankind stuck and spinning around in circles for centuries and getting nowhere. Now, in Rebuilding the Village, he rouses our imaginations to consider a whole new set of possibilities, and offers an alternative framework, new way of thinking, and set of tools for birthing that new world together. Ken Dahl's dream is not a pipe dream; it has real substance and teeth to it."

Religion's character sketch of humanity is NOT the same as what the actual facts, statistics, and observable reality clearly reveal about humanity. This book covers everything from theological and philosophical concepts that have governed our global thinking, to cultural and environmental realities we need to start talking about, to the very unnatural commerce systems our world operates on. This book shows where we came from, how it happened, and how history is vividly showing credible, statistic-based data (even amidst our greatest problems) of how our world is changing for the better, and some real, practical solutions of how humankind WILL eventually achieve global peace and brotherhood.

Book #4. THE BURST OF THUNDER IN YOUR EAR

There is a familiar phrase that says, "Things are not always what they seem." As I grew older I began to notice just the opposite to be true. The phrase should have read, "Things are not always what they have been taught to be." Throughout our lives we are often faced with small philosophical adjustments. We humbly change beliefs that we once so confidently held into newer, more accurate-to-reality versions. Hopefully this moves us in a more positive direction. But then, sometimes, like a violent burst of thunder - we are suddenly forced to rethink some of the very foundational beliefs we inherited from those we love and trust the most.

There is a time for a hundred small steps, and a time for a dozen really large steps. Then there are bold and daring paradigm shifts. The Burst of Thunder in Your Ear is about those whose journeys of radical theological shifts are now moving them from some of the more traditional teachings of old to some of today's more progressive thinking, concepts, and observations.

The idea that the old information is "all the information" is simply not true. Every generation has proven this. Ours will be no exception. The reason some of the things our culture has taught us never did seem to make logical sense is simply because they *don't* make logical sense. And the reason we were not able to pursue those intuitive moments is because we were also taught not to trust our own attributes of intuition, logic, deductive reasoning, or even common sense. In fact, many have been taught that those inbuilt attributes are actually "dangerous" to rely on...

If the "band you're in" is starting to "play different tunes," then this could be the book in which you say, "Oh Dorothy, there's no coming back from this."

Visit Ken's Facebook page at facebook.com/kendahlbooks
All paperbacks and Kindle versions available on amazon.com

Made in the USA
San Bernardino, CA
16 December 2016